SELF-CONFIDENCE FOR WOMEN

Step by step for successful life

TABLE OF CONTENTS

CHAPTER 1
Why Women Are an Important Portion of Society?

Job of Ladies in The General Public

Women are the essential piece of the general public. Amazing changes have occurred over the world lately, however the status and destiny of ladies has not changed a lot. In Pakistan, their circumstance has gotten a lot of more terrible.

We were as of late evaluated as one of the most exceedingly awful nations on the planet with regards to the manner in which we treat ladies. Over 60 years after freedom, 80 percent of Pakistani ladies are still exposed to abusive behavior at home. Our nation is positioned 82 out of 93 nations on the Gender Development Index and 152 out of 156 nations on the Gender Empowerment Measure. We are additionally among a bunch of nations where there is a negative sex proportion of 100 ladies to 108 men. Despite the fact that ladies can possibly assume a multidimensional job from cultural to authoritative, yet they have been disregarded. Our nation's backwardness can straightforwardly be ascribed to the precluded job from securing ladies in nation's improvement.

Quaid-e-Azam said in discourse in 1944:

"No country can ascend to the tallness of greatness except if your ladies are next to each other with you; we are casualties of underhandedness customs. It is an unspeakable atrocity that our ladies are quieted down inside the four dividers of the houses as detainees".

Man centric men disapprove of training for ladies. Not just this, numerous ladies are additionally denied the open door for work and gain vocation. Their word related decisions are restricted because of social and social limitations and inalienable sex inclination in the work showcase. They likewise need steady offices, for example, childcare, transport and convenience in the conventional segment of the work showcase. Ladies' work control is viewed as sub-par in light of manager's foreordained idea of ladies' essential job as homemakers. Because of separation, their job is low paid and prompts absence of potential upward versatility.

Notwithstanding, the Prophet Mohammad (PBUH) emphatically underlined on training by saying that, "It is the prime obligation of people to procure instruction".

Islam is a complete religion that gives ladies an extraordinary significance. Be that as it may, the intolerant and one-sided strict Ulemas have consistently misconstrued it to fill their devilish needs. It adds up to disregard the genuine soul of Islam that gives ladies equity in each circle of life.

Ladies can assume a more prominent job in the advancement of our country. They have an extraordinary potential to lift our country, which is overflowing with issues. God has gave them with all abilities and their job in any circle whether it is social, financial, political, social or instructive can't be disregarded. We have to use their ability in correct place and concede their stake in nation's advancement.

Ladies of Pakistan are exceptionally dedicated towards their job in the improvement of the nation and they are developing as striking individuals from the general public.

The Role of Women in Society Essay

Ladies are significant in our general public. Each lady has her own activity or obligation in this cutting edge society wherein men are as yet the 'most grounded sexual orientation';. We can't overlook such ladies' reality is much more convoluted than a man's life. A lady needs to deal with her very own life and on the off chance that she is a mother , she needs to take care likewise about her kids' life as well. Marriaged ladies have heaps of stresses and in all honesty , they complete a more stressfull life than marriaged men.

A few times throughout my life I have heard editorials about the absence of significance of ladies. I am by and by against these sort of editorials. In my life the most notable individual I recall is my mom. She is an expert likewise , ... show increasingly content...

At home the most notable individual is in the greater part of the cases is the mother. She is the one that thinks about the request , the issue and the strength of all the family. Be that as it may, the stresses she convey for us are not absolutely extrange. They care such a great amount for us in light of the fact that in all honesty , we were a piece of her right around nine months and now , as we grow up , we are the connection that will give our parent's gens the oportunity of living for another age. Likewise , we can see that the man of the house has different stresses, for example, how to fund-raise enough to bolster his family the whole week. Hence he can't acomplish the considerations that the lady of the house takes with their very own youngsters.

By and by , I can't envision my existence without the picture and the help of my mom. I accept that a mother is the 80 % of the consideration you ever will require. I am and I will be the individual I am a direct result of my mom. I am certain that the main thing I may miss if some time or another I free my family could be my mom and this is the ideal opportunity when I understand and persuade myself that she is the most notable individual for me . I am certain my remark could be acknowledged by the majority of the individuals living in a comparable society.

Besides, they are advancing the reason for ladies' status and job in the general public. It must be conceded and extolled that these brave ladies have not just made mindfulness among the kindred ladies about their quality and significance, yet have additionally installed themselves into the stages where their requests could meet achievement. Presently the opportunity has arrived to effectively coordinate them in nations undertakings with the goal that we can quicker the pace of progress of Pakistan. The errand is straightforward and ladies need to turn out from the shackles of male prevalence.

The Place of Women in Our Society or The Duties of Women

Ladies assume a fundamental job in human advance and have a huge spot in the general public. They are not under any condition second rate compared to men. They are fit for sharing every one of the duties of life. Man and lady have been appropriately contrasted with the wheels of a similar carriage.

Islam has concurred an equivalent situation to ladies in the general public. Islam understood the significance of ladies and allowed them an extremely noble position equivalent to man. The principle duty of a lady is to save humankind. As a mother, her position is one of a kind. She raises the kids with extraordinary consideration. The primary school of a kid is the lap of his mom. It is very evident that incredible man had extraordinary moms.

Napoleon stated: "Give me great moms and I will give you a decent country." The advancement of country relies on the manner in which the moms raise their kids. On the off chance that the moms are instructed, the entire society will advance. Ladies have constantly assumed a significant job in the advancement of a country.

In the beginning of Islam, ladies worked next to each other with men. In the combat zone, they breast fed the harmed, kept up the provisions and in specific cases even battled fearlessly. Florence Nightingale was the lady, who drove an exceptionally fruitful crusade for the changes of medical clinics and nursing calling. Ladies had been extraordinary holy people, researchers, artists, authors, reformers and directors. Ladies ought to be given appropriate instruction and preparing. They should comprehended what life is and how it ought to be lived.

Instructed ladies can do a lot to change the general public. Numerous unsettling influences in the general public is made by those enemy of social people, who were raised by wrong hands. In present day age, ladies are going very well in every one of the fields of progress. They are exhibiting their gifts in best. They are filling in as instructors, specialists, Engineers, Administrators and even leader of the states. The proficiency rate among the ladies so in Pakistan is low. The need is to expand this proportion. More instruction among the ladies implies the more advancement of the general public.

Sex Equality

About 3000 understudies, guardians, instructors, young men and young ladies, took an interest in a 16 Days cyclothon and walkathon in India in 2016 as a feature of the Orange The World crusade initiated by UN Women, to bring issues to light of sexual orientation based viciousness.

The incomplete business within recent memory

Ladies and young ladies speak to half of the total populace and, in this way, additionally 50% of its latent capacity. Sex uniformity, other than being a central human right, is basic to accomplish tranquil social orders, with full human potential and reasonable improvement. Besides, it has been indicated that engaging ladies spikes profitability and monetary development.

Tragically, there is as yet far to go to accomplish full balance of rights and openings among people, cautions UN Women. Along these lines, it is of foremost significance to end the various types of sexual orientation savagery and secure equivalent access to quality training and wellbeing, financial assets and cooperation in political life for the two ladies and young ladies and men and young men. It is additionally fundamental to accomplish equivalent open doors in access to work and to places of authority and basic leadership at all levels.

The UN Secretary-General, Mr. António Guterres has expressed that accomplishing sexual orientation fairness and enabling ladies and young ladies is the incomplete business within recent memory, and the best human rights challenge in our reality.

The United Nations and ladies

UN support for the privileges of ladies started with the Organization's establishing Charter. Among the reasons for the UN announced in Article 1 of its Charter is "To accomplish global co-activity ... in advancing and empowering regard for human rights and for crucial opportunities for all without qualification as to race, sex, language, or religion."

Inside the UN's first year, the Economic and Social Council built up its Commission on the Status of Women, as the key worldwide approach making body devoted solely to sex equity and progression of ladies. Among its most punctual achievements was guaranteeing unbiased language in the draft Universal Declaration of Human Rights.

Ladies and human rights

The milestone Declaration, embraced by the General Assembly on 10 December 1948, reaffirms that "Every person are brought into the world free and equivalent in respect and rights" and that "everybody is qualified for every one of the rights and opportunities set out in this Declaration, without qualification of any sort, for example, race, shading, sex, language, religion, ... birth or different status."

As the universal women's activist development started to pick up force during the 1970s, the General Assembly pronounced

1975 as the International Women's Year and sorted out the primary World Conference on Women, held in Mexico City. At the asking of the Conference, it accordingly proclaimed the years 1976-1985 as the UN Decade for Women, and built up a Voluntary Fund for Decade.

In 1979, the General Assembly received the Convention on the Elimination of All Forms of Discrimination against Women (CEDAW), which is frequently depicted as an International Bill of Rights for Women. In its 30 articles, the Convention expressly characterizes victimization ladies and sets up a motivation for national activity to end such separation. The Convention targets culture and custom as compelling powers molding sex jobs and family relations, and it is the principal human rights settlement to certify the regenerative privileges of ladies.

Five years after the Mexico City meeting, a Second World Conference on Women was held in Copenhagen in 1980. The subsequent Program of Action called for more grounded national measures to guarantee ladies' possession and control of property, just as upgrades in ladies' privileges regarding legacy, youngster guardianship and loss of nationality.

Birth of Global Feminism

In 1985, the World Conference to Review and Appraise the Achievements of the United

Nations Decade for Women: Equality, Development and Peace, was held in Nairobi. It was met when the development for sexual orientation correspondence had at long last increased genuine worldwide acknowledgment, and 15,000 agents of non-administrative associations (NGOs) took part in a parallel NGO Forum.

The occasion was depicted by numerous individuals as "the introduction of worldwide woman's rights". Understanding that the objectives of the Mexico City Conference had not been enough met, the 157 partaking governments received the Nairobi Forward-looking Strategies to the Year 2000. The record kicked off something new by pronouncing all issues to be ladies' issues.

Beijing Conference on Women

The Fourth World Conference on Women, held in Beijing in 1995, went above and beyond than the Nairobi Conference. The Beijing Platform for Action stated ladies' privileges as human rights and focused on explicit activities to guarantee regard for those rights.

Commission on the Status of Women

The Commission on the Status of Women (CSW) is the key worldwide intergovernmental body solely committed to the advancement of sex fairness and the strengthening of ladies. The CSW is instrumental in advancing ladies' privileges, recording the truth of ladies' lives all through the world, and molding worldwide measures on sexual orientation correspondence and the strengthening of ladies.

An Organization for ladies

On 2 July 2010, the United Nations General Assembly collectively casted a ballot to make a solitary UN body entrusted with quickening progress in accomplishing sexual orientation uniformity and ladies' strengthening. The new UN Entity for Gender Equality and the Empowerment of Women – or UN Women – blended four of the world body's offices and workplaces: the UN Development Fund for Women (UNIFEM), the Division for the Advancement of Women (DAW), the Office of the Special Adviser on Gender Issues, and the UN International Research and Training Institute for the Advancement of Women.

Ladies and the Sustainable Development Goals

Sex correspondence

The United Nations is currently concentrating its worldwide improvement deal with the as of late created 17 Sustainable Development Goals (SDGs). Ladies have a basic task to carry out in the entirety of the SDGs, with numerous objectives explicitly perceiving ladies' balance and strengthening as both the goal, and as a feature of the arrangement.

Objective 5, to "Accomplish sex correspondence and enable all ladies and young ladies" is known as the independent sex objective, since it is committed to accomplishing these closures. Profound lawful and authoritative changes are expected to guarantee ladies' privileges far and wide. While a record 143 nations ensured fairness among people in their Constitutions by 2014, another 52 had not made this stride.

Distinct sex abberations stay in financial and political domains. While there has been some advancement throughout the decades, all things considered ladies in the work advertise still acquire 20 percent not as much as men comprehensively. Starting at 2018, just 24 percent of every single national parliamentarian were female, a moderate ascent from 11.3 percent in 1995.

Wiping out Violence Against Women

The UN framework keeps on giving specific thoughtfulness regarding the issue of brutality against ladies. The 1993 General Assembly Declaration on the Elimination of Violence against Women contained "a reasonable and exhaustive meaning of viciousness against ladies [and] an unmistakable articulation of the rights to be applied to guarantee the disposal of brutality against ladies in the entirety of its structures". It spoke to "a dedication by States in regard of their duties, and a responsibility by the worldwide network everywhere to the end of brutality against ladies".

Savagery against ladies is a pandemic influencing all nations, even those that have gained commendable ground in different regions. Around the world, 35 percent of ladies have encountered either physical as well as sexual personal accomplice brutality or non-accomplice sexual viciousness.

In September 2017, the European Union and the United Nations united to dispatch the Spotlight Initiative, a worldwide, multi-year activity that spotlights on killing all types of savagery against ladies and young ladies.

The International Day for the Elimination of Violence against Women is seen on 25 November.

Ladies' Day and different observances

Universal Women's Day is watched every year on 8 March. Worldwide Women's Day originally rose up out of the exercises of work developments at the turn of the twentieth century in North America and crosswise over Europe. It is a day, saw by numerous nations around the globe, on which ladies are perceived for their accomplishments regardless of divisions, whether national, ethnic, phonetic, social, monetary or political.

Other than International Women's Day and the International Day for the Elimination of Violence against Women, the UN watches other global days devoted to bringing issues to light of various parts of the battle for sexual orientation correspondence and ladies strengthening. On February 6, the International Day of Zero Tolerance to Female Genital Mutilation is watched, February 11 is the International Day of Women and Girls in Science, June 19 is the International Day for the Elimination of Sexual Violence in Conflict, June 23 is International Widows' Day, October 11 is the International Day of the Girl Child and on October 15 the International Day of Rural Women is watched.

Sexual orientation Inclusive Language GuidelinesGender-comprehensive language

Given the key job that language plays in molding social and social frames of mind, utilizing sex comprehensive language is a ground-breaking approach to advance sex uniformity and destroy sexual orientation predisposition.

Being comprehensive from a sexual orientation language point of view implies talking and writing in a manner that doesn't victimize a specific sex, social sex or sex character, and doesn't sustain sex generalizations.

Ladies' investment in all parts of society more fundamental than any other time in recent memory – UN authorities

Universal Women's Day 2012: balance starts at home for provincial young ladies and women.IFAD

Universal Women's Day 2012: balance starts at home for provincial young ladies and ladies. Ladies' voices and their investment in all parts of society are a higher priority than any time in recent memory, as saw a year ago with regards to the worldwide financial emergency, political changes in the Arab world and somewhere else, and ecological debacles, United Nations authorities focused on today as they checked International Women's Day.

Ladies' voices and their investment in all parts of society are a higher priority than any time in recent memory, as saw a year ago with regards to the worldwide financial emergency, political advances in the Arab world and somewhere else, and ecological debacles, United Nations authorities focused on today as they stamped International Women's Day.

Michelle Bachelet, Executive Director of the UN Entity for Gender Equality and the Empowerment of Women (UN Women), who made a trip to Morocco to commend the Day, featured the job of ladies in the midst of the political changes in the Arab district, and approached world pioneers to propel ladies' inclusion in legislative issues and enable them financially.

"In spite of the means taken forward and the advancement made in numerous Arab States, ladies are requesting more prominent advancement," she said during a question and answer session in Rabat. "The differentiation of having the world's least portrayal of ladies in legislative issues and the work power gives neither equity to Arab ladies nor to the history, inheritance and eventual fate of the Arab world," she said.

UN Independent Expert Kamala Chandrakirana, who heads another gathering accused of distinguishing approaches to dispose of existing separation rehearses against ladies, resounded Ms. Bachelet's comments, cautioning that financial and political changes are a critical time to propel ladies' privileges yet cautioned that they are additionally in danger.

"In political progress, there is a risk of relapse in the delight by ladies of their human rights and ladies taking part in open life are regularly presented to savagery," Ms. Chandrakirana said. "States must accept the open door of political progress to improve ladies' protected and political position, receiving positive measures to take out separation and advance the strengthening of ladies."

She likewise focused on that the effect of a financial emergency is particularly cruel for ladies "because of dubious business, decrease in government managed savings and crumbling in the consideration economy."

Ladies are likewise progressively defenseless during cataclysmic events, and the Secretary-General's Special Representative for Disaster Risk Reduction, Margareta Wahlström, focused on that nations need to instruct ladies to have the option to confront them and to construct strength in the network all in all.

"Ladies' lives are placed in peril since they are dealt with like peons in the absolute most danger inclined locales of the world," she said. "There is solid proof to propose that ladies are bound to bite the dust in a debacles than men and it is regularly on the grounds that they are denied access to essential data about fiasco hazard and repressed by social standards from getting away from the home or working environment to maintain a strategic distance from death."

In his message to stamp the Day, Secretary-General Ban Ki-moon noticed that, from access to training and rights to land proprietorship, to political cooperation and equivalent compensation, ladies still linger behind men even in nations where there have been huge endeavors to address sex imbalances.

"Sexual orientation fairness and the strengthening of ladies are making strides around the world" he stated, while cautioning that "in spite of this energy, there is far to go before ladies and young ladies can be said to appreciate the major rights, opportunity and pride that are their bequest and that will ensure their prosperity." He underlined that nations ought to wipe out biased laws and practices that have a negative impact on ladies as well as on whole networks and countries.

Inconsistent treatment of ladies can bring about more extensive issues that influence social orders in general. For instance, the UN High Commissioner for Refugees (UNHCR) cautioned that laws in 25 nations that don't enable ladies to present nationality on their kids take steps to leave a large number of people in a condition of statelessness. At present, there are about 12 million individuals around the globe who are not considered as nationals of any state, of whom half are youngsters.

"A kid brought into the world stateless today faces an eventual fate of vulnerability and weakness," said Erika Feller, UNHCR's Assistant High Commissioner for Protection. "When there is separation in giving nationality, we see kids getting stateless from the minute they're conceived."

The current year's subject for the Afternoon, 'Engage Rural Women — End Hunger and

Poverty,' centers around giving chances to the absolute least fortunate ladies around the globe. The UN's International Fund for Agricultural Development (IFAD), World Food Program (WFP) and Food and Agriculture Organization (FAO) composed an exchange with different specialists that concentrated on this specific issue.

"It is essential that open venture, administrations and arrangements for agribusiness and rustic improvement be arranged and executed thinking about the various jobs, intrigue and chances of ladies and men as ranchers and rural specialists," said Carlos Seré, IFAD Chief Development Strategist.

In the interim, the Joint UN Program on HIV/AIDS (UNAIDS) focused on that ladies are key in the worldwide battle against the destructive illness. "There are scarcely any supportable arrangements that empower ladies and young ladies to shield themselves from HIV, viciousness and neediness," UNAIDS stated, including that "engaged ladies and young ladies are basic specialists of progress in turning around the scourge."

The Day was seen in different pieces of the world, from Afghanistan to Sudan. The UN Assistance Mission in Afghanistan (UNAMA) featured its report on dispensing with brutality against ladies, which found both positive advancement and holes in the usage of the pertinent law in the nation. The report noticed that despite the fact that law authorization is improving, there is far to go before Afghan ladies are completely shielded from brutality.

In Somalia, the Secretary-General's Special Representative, Augustine P. Mahiga, highlighted the ongoing additions made towards expanding ladies' portrayal in the continuous harmony process in the nation through the guide, which urges ladies and youth to participate in the political fate of the nation.

As a component of the festivals for the Afternoon, the UN Population Fund (UNFPA) opened a presentation at UN Headquarters in New York exhibiting blankets made by ladies everywhere throughout the world that show amazing messages and offers for activity.

Also, Mr. Boycott and the President of the General Assembly, Nassir Abdulaziz Al-Nasser, have proposed the gathering of a worldwide meeting on ladies in 2015 – 20 years after the last ladies' summit in Beijing.

Arriving at CHILDREN'S POTENTIAL

From the beginning of time, the focal job of ladies in the public eye has guaranteed the steadiness, advance and long haul improvement of countries.

Comprehensively, ladies involve 43 percent of the world's rural work power – ascending to

70 percent in certain nations. For example, crosswise over Africa, 80 percent of the horticultural creation originates from little ranchers, the greater part of whom are country ladies. It's generally acknowledged that farming can be the motor of development and destitution decrease in creating countries. Ladies, prominently moms, assume the biggest job in basic leadership about family supper arranging and diet. What's more, ladies self-report all the more frequently their drive in protecting youngster wellbeing and sustenance.

Job of Ladies in India

The Role of Women as Caretakers

Ladies are the essential guardians of kids and older folks in each nation of the world. Worldwide examinations show that when the economy and political association of a general public change, ladies lead the pack in helping the family conform to new substances and difficulties. They are probably going to be the prime initiator of outside help, and assume a significant job in encouraging (or frustrating) changes in family life.

"Rustic ladies assume a key job in supporting their family units and networks in accomplishing nourishment and sustenance security, producing salary, and improving provincial employments and in general prosperity."

– UN Womenwatch Organization

The Role of Women as Educators

The commitment of ladies to a general public's change from pre-educated to proficient in like manner is verifiable. Fundamental instruction is vital to a country's capacity to create and accomplish manageability targets. Research has demonstrated that instruction can improve farming efficiency, upgrade the status of young ladies and ladies, lessen populace development rates, upgrade ecological insurance, and generally increase the expectation of living.

It is the mother in the family who frequently encourages offspring of the two sexual orientations to visit – and remain – in school. The job of ladies is at the front finish of the chain of upgrades prompting the family's, the network's long haul limit.

Job of Women in St. Lucia

The Role of Women in the Workforce

Today, the middle female portion of the worldwide workforce is 45.4 percent. Ladies' formal and casual work can change a network from a moderately self-ruling society to a member in the national economy. Regardless of huge hindrances, ladies' independent companies in country creating networks not exclusively can be a more distant family's life saver, however can frame an arranged financial establishment for people in the future. The job of ladies in the urban and country workforce has extended exponentially in ongoing decades.

Job of Ladies in China

The topic for International Women's Day 2019 "Think equivalent, form brilliant, advance for change," was picked to distinguish inventive approaches to propel sex correspondence and the strengthening of ladies, quickening the 2030 Agenda, gathering speed for the powerful usage of the new U.N. Manageable Development Goals. Obviously, ladies' chances still linger behind those of men around the world. In any case, the noteworthy and current job of ladies is undeniable.

"At the point when ladies are enabled and can guarantee their privileges and access to land, administration, openings and decisions, economies develop, nourishment security is upgraded and prospects are improved for present and people in the future."

– Michelle Bachelet, Under-Secretary-General and Executive Director of UN Women

The Role of Women as Global Volunteers

Worldwide Volunteers' people group advancement work in have nations overall fortifies ladies' and kids' ability and supports their continued wellbeing and improvement. Under the course of neighborhood pioneers, our volunteers help guarantee scholastic availability, cultivate parental inclusion, offer psycho-social help, give sustenance and wellbeing instruction, support young ladies' grants, develop schools with young ladies' restrooms, coach education, and numeracy, thus considerably more. Get in touch with us utilizing the structure underneath to figure out how you can add to this basic motivation. At the point when more ladies join the workforce, everybody benefits. Here's the reason

Liz Azoulay, 26, who stacks and empties freight at Ashdod port, models for a photo at the port, in Ashdod, southern Israel, February 22, 2017. "In the vast majority of my expert life I didn't confront any imbalance. In the port of Ashdod we are equivalent on the docks. I am the main lady who started working at the Ashdod port as a stevedore." REUTERS/Amir Cohen SEARCH "Ladies WORK" FOR THIS STORY. SEARCH "More extensive IMAGE" FOR ALL STORIES. - RC19E4D97240

In spite of some advancement, the holes in labor power cooperation among people stay enormous. To take only one model, no progressed or center salary economy has diminished the sexual orientation hole underneath 7 rate focuses.

This lopsided playing field among ladies and men comes at a huge financial expense as it hampers efficiency and burdens development. An ongoing IMF staff study finds that hindrances to ladies entering the work power—consider charge bends, segregation, and social and social components—are costlier than recommended by past research and the advantages from shutting sexual orientation holes are much bigger than thought previously. Policymakers ought to consequently concentrate on evacuating such obstructions desperately.

Sex decent variety matters

Our investigation springs from the perception—bolstered by impressive microeconomic proof—that ladies and men carry various abilities and points of view to the work environment, including various demeanors to hazard and joint effort. Studies have additionally demonstrated that the money related execution of firms improves with more sex equivalent corporate sheets.

Shockingly, past investigations have not taken a gander at the macroeconomic ramifications of this smaller scale proof.

In the standard course reading examination, the work power is the aggregate of the headcounts of male and female specialists. Since supplanting a man by a lady in this aggregate doesn't influence the work power, there are no increases from sexual orientation assorted variety: people are thought to be superbly substitutable.

Advantages from shutting sexual orientation holes are considerably bigger than recently suspected.

However, our proof—from macroeconomic, sectoral, and firm-level information—shows that ladies and men supplement each other in the generation procedure, making an extra profit by expanding ladies' work on development. As it were, adding more ladies to the work power ought to bring bigger financial additions than an equivalent increment in male specialists (mirroring the way that, in market analysts' language, the flexibility of substitution among ladies and men underway is low).

Key advantages from narrowing sexual orientation holes

The ramifications of this discovering are huge.

A greater lift to development: Because ladies carry new aptitudes to the work environment, the efficiency and development gains from adding ladies to the work power (by decreasing hindrances to ladies' investment in the work power) are bigger than recently suspected. Without a doubt, our alignment practice recommends that, for the base portion of the nations in our example as far as sexual orientation disparity, shutting the sex hole could expand GDP by a normal of 35 percent. Four fifths of these increases originate from adding laborers to the work power, however completely one fifth of the additions are because of the sex decent variety impact on profitability.

Higher profitability: When translating past information in circumstances where the sexual orientation hole has been narrowing after some time, the commitment to development from improved proficiency (or absolute factor efficiency gains) is exaggerated. A segment of the addition ascribed to profitability is in reality because of the expanded interest of ladies after some time.

Higher male salaries: Our outcomes propose that men's wages will likewise increment because of more noteworthy incorporation of ladies in the work power since profitability will increment. This is significant in light of the fact that these higher wages ought to reinforce support for evacuating obstructions that keep ladies away from OK work.

Have you perused?

At the point when sexual orientation imbalance is great financial matters

Is this why we've not accomplished sexual orientation balance at work?

The sex pay hole stretches to the lowest pay permitted by law laborers as well

A greater result to decreasing sex hindrances along advancement ways: The ascent of the administrations division driven by financial improvement carries more ladies into the work power. In any case, our work demonstrates that boundaries to ladies' business moderate this procedure. These hindrances change crosswise over districts and nations, and are enormous in certain pieces of the world—equal to assess rates on ladies' work of up to 50 percent. What's more, the relating welfare misfortunes (which consider utilization and relaxation time) are enormous, in any event, while taking into consideration the way that "home generation" is decreased when ladies enter the work power. For instance, we find that welfare costs surpass 20 percent in the

Middle East and North Africa locale and in South Asia.

Receiving the rewards

While there is no silver projectile, there are a few strategies that can help slender sexual orientation holes. These incorporate instituting laws to guarantee that ladies have equivalent rights to possess property and access credit. Changing charges (for instance, by supplanting family tax collection with singular tax collection and giving assessment credits) can boost work power interest among low-salary workers. Handling sexual orientation imbalance in instruction and human services, including freely financed maternity and paternity leave, extended childcare, and senior consideration accessibility can expand ladies' interest in the work advertise. Improving access to transportation, power, and water foundation can likewise help lift ladies' cooperation in the workforce.

The comprehensive view

These are not every new concern, yet there is a restored desire to move quickly. For a considerable length of time, the IMF has been at the cutting edge of strategy investigation featuring the financial expenses of disparity and potential cures. We realize that the unlevel playing field among ladies and men has considerable financial expenses and can obstruct the monetary wellbeing of countries.

We are currently discovering that these expenses are considerably bigger than we suspected. Since we see the full picture, the case for more prominent sexual orientation value has gotten much all the more convincing.

CHAPTER 2

What is self confidence

The confidence development has moved through Western culture in the course of recent years, with guardians and instructors the same multiplying down on the possibility that improving youngsters' self-assurance will prompt improved execution, and a progressively fruitful life when all is said in done (Baskin, 2011).

This development began with a book distributed in 1969, in which clinician Nathaniel Branden contended that generally mental or passionate issues individuals confronted could be followed back to low confidence. Branden established the framework for the Self-Esteem Movement with his declaration that improving a person's confidence couldn't just bring about better execution yet could even fix pathology.

From that point forward, there have been a great many papers distributed and contemplates directed on the connection among progress and confidence. This is a famous thought in writing as well as in more standard mediums also. Before we start investigating the complexities of confidence it is fundamental to unload the contrasts between the covering ideas of self-viability, fearlessness, and confidence.

"When we have confidence in ourselves, we can chance interest, wonder, unconstrained pleasure, or any experience that uncovers the human soul."

– E.E. Cummings

This article contains:

Characterizing the Difference: Self-Efficacy, Self-Confidence, and Self-Esteem

Well known Theories of Self-Confidence

The Importance of Self-Confidence

A lot of Good Thing: The Unintended Consequences of Self-Esteem Education

The Benefits of Fear: Practicing Courage and Building Confidence

9 Lessons for Practicing Self-Confidence

Bring Home Message: It's a Process

References

Characterizing the Difference: Self-Efficacy, Self-Confidence, and Self-Esteem

While the vast majority for the most part consider confidence and fearlessness as two names for something very similar, and presumably seldom consider the expression "self-viability," these three terms hold marginally various implications for the analysts who study them (Druckman and Bjork, 1994; Oney, and Oksuzoglu-Guven, 2015).

What is Self-Efficacy?

Albert Bandura is seemingly the most refered to creator regarding the matter of self-adequacy, and he characterizes self-viability as a person's convictions about their ability to impact the occasions in their very own lives (Bandura, 1977).

This varies from confidence in a significant manner: the meaning of confidence regularly lays on thoughts regarding a person's worth or value, while self-viability is established in convictions about a person's capacities to deal with future circumstances. In this sense, confidence is all the more a present-centered conviction while self-adequacy is to a greater degree a forward-looking conviction.

What is Self-Confidence?

This is likely the most utilized term for these related ideas outside of mental research, yet there is still some perplexity about what precisely self-assurance is. One of the most refered to sources about fearlessness alludes to it as essentially putting stock in oneself (Bénabou and Tirole, 2002). Another well known article characterizes fearlessness as a person's desires for execution and self-assessments of capacities and earlier execution (Lenney, 1977).

At long last, Psychology Dictionary Online characterizes self-assurance as a person's trust in their very own capacities, limits, and decisions, or conviction that the person can effectively confront everyday difficulties and requests (Psychology Dictionary Online).

Self-assurance additionally achieves more bliss. Normally, when you are positive about your capacities you are more joyful because of your victories. At the point when you are resting easy thinking about your capacities, the more empowered and roused you are to make a move and accomplish your objectives.

Self-assurance, at that point, is like self-adequacy in that it will in general spotlight on the person's future execution; in any case, it is by all accounts dependent on earlier execution, thus one might say, it additionally centers around the past.

Numerous clinicians will in general allude to self-viability while considering a person's convictions about their capacities concerning a particular assignment or set of undertakings, while fearlessness is all the more frequently alluded to as a more extensive and increasingly stable attribute concerning a person's view of by and large ability.

What is Self-Esteem?

The most compelling voices in confidence examine were, seemingly, Morris Rosenberg and Nathaniel Branden. In his 1965 book, Society and the Adolescent Self-Image,

Rosenberg talked about his interpretation of confidence and presented his broadly utilized acknowledged Self-Esteem Scale.

A Free PDF of the Rosenberg's Self-Esteem Scale is accessible here.

His meaning of confidence laid on the supposition that it was a moderately steady conviction about one's general self-esteem. This is an expansive meaning of confidence, characterizing it as a quality that is affected by various factors and is generally hard to change.

Interestingly, Branden trusts confidence is comprised of two unmistakable segments: self-adequacy, or the certainty we have in our capacity to adapt to life's difficulties, and sense of pride, or the conviction that we are meriting bliss, love, and achievement (1969). The definitions are comparative, however it is significant that Rosenberg's definition depends on convictions about self-esteem, a conviction which can have fiercely various implications to various individuals, while Branden is progressively explicit about which convictions are engaged with confidence.

Shouldn't something be said about the individuals who have an excess of confidence? Narcissism is simply the aftereffect of having an excessive amount of regard. A mental definition would be an outrageous measure of narrow-mindedness, with a self important perspective on one's own gifts and a hankering for deference.

Confidence at high and low levels can be harming so it is imperative to find some kind of harmony in the center. A reasonable however positive perspective on oneself is frequently perfect.

Where does confidence originate from? What impact does it have on our lives? Confidence is frequently observed as a character characteristic, which implies it will in general be steady and persevering.

There are commonly three segments which make up confidence:

Confidence is a basic human need that is fundamental for endurance and ordinary, solid advancement

Confidence emerges consequently from inside dependent on an individual's convictions and cognizance

Confidence happens related to an individual's musings, practices, sentiments, and activities.

Confidence is one of the fundamental human inspirations in Abraham Maslow's progression of necessities. Maslow would propose that people need both regard from others just as internal identity regard. These necessities must be satisfied all together for a person to develop and flourish.

These requirements must be satisfied all together for a person to develop and accomplish self-realization. Fearlessness and confidence are two firmly related mental wonders, both dependent on past encounters and both looking forward at future execution.

Going ahead, with an end goal to downplay perplexity, we will believe self-assurance and confidence to be basically a similar idea.

We investigate this further in The Science of Self-Acceptance Masterclass©

Well known Theories of Self-Confidence

With these definitions close by, we can investigate basic convictions and well known speculations encircle self-assurance and confidence.

As noted before, Branden's hypothesis of confidence turned into a broadly referenced and got hypothesis, yet there were additionally different speculations and structures for understanding confidence in the mental writing.

Maslow's Hierarchy of Needs

Maslow's pecking order of necessities, a notorious albeit to some degree obsolete structure in brain research, estimates that there are a few needs that people more likely than not met to be really satisfied, yet, by and large, the most essential needs should be met before increasingly complex needs can be met (1943). In his pyramid, confidence is the second most significant level of need, simply under self-completion.

As per Maslow, people must have their needs of physiological dependability, security, love and having a place met before they can create sound confidence. He additionally noticed that there are two sorts of confidence, a "higher" and a "lower," the lower confidence got from the regard of others, while the higher confidence originates from inside.

In the years following his presentation of the pecking order of necessities, Maslow refined his hypothesis to suit the examples of profoundly self-completed individuals who are destitute or people who live in a hazardous region or combat area but at the same time are high in confidence.

This pecking order is never again considered as an exacting hypothesis of unidirectional development, however a progressively broad clarification of how fundamental needs being met permit people the opportunity and capacity to accomplish their increasingly intricate ones.

Fear Management Theory

A darker hypothesis that dives somewhat more profound into the human experience to account for self-assurance is the Terror Management Theory.

Fear Management Theory (TMT) depends on the possibility that people hold extraordinary potential for reacting with dread to the attention to their very own mortality, and that perspectives that accentuate people groups' convictions in their very own importance as people secure them against this fear (Greenberg and Arndt, 2011).

TMT places that confidence frames as an approach to ensure and cushion against uneasiness, and consequently individuals take a stab at fearlessness and respond adversely to anybody or anything that could undermine their convictions in their soothing perspective.

Sociometer Theory

Imprint Leary, a social analyst who looks into confidence with regards to developmental brain research, likewise contributed a hypothesis of confidence to the writing.

The Sociometer Theory proposes that confidence is an interior measure of how much one is incorporated versus prohibited by others (Leary, 2006). This hypothesis lays on the origination of confidence as an inward individual view of social acknowledgment and dismissal.

WHAT IS SELF-CONFIDENCE?

Fearlessness is a disposition about your aptitudes and capacities. It implies you acknowledge and confide in yourself and have a feeling of control in your life. You know your qualities and shortcoming admirably, and have a positive perspective on yourself. You set practical desires and objectives, impart decisively, and can deal with analysis.

Then again, low self-assurance may make you feel brimming with self-question, be aloof or compliant, or experience issues confiding in others. You may feel sub-par, disliked, or be delicate to analysis. Feeling certain about yourself may rely upon the circumstance. For example, you can feel sure about certain territories, for example, scholastics, however need trust in others, similar to connections.

Having high or low fearlessness is once in a while identified with your real capacities, and for the most part dependent on your recognitions. Discernments are simply the manner in which your think and these contemplations can be imperfect.

Low self-assurance may originate from various encounters, for example, experiencing childhood in an unsupportive and basic condition, being isolated from your companions or family just because, making a decision about yourself too brutally, or fearing disappointment. Individuals with low self-assurance regularly have mistakes in their reasoning.

Instructions to Increase Your Self-Confidence

- Perceive and accentuate your qualities. Prize and recognition yourself for your endeavors and progress.

- At the point when you unearth an obstruction, treat yourself with graciousness and sympathy. Try not to harp on disappointment.

- Set sensible and reachable objectives. Try not to anticipate flawlessness; it is difficult to be impeccable in each part of life.

- Slow down when you are feeling serious feelings and contemplate the circumstance.

- Challenge making suspicions about yourself, individuals and circumstances.

- Perceive that past negative beneficial encounters don't direct your future.

- Express your sentiments, convictions and needs straightforwardly and deferentially

- Figure out how to disapprove of outlandish solicitations.

Building Self-Confidence

Setting yourself up for Success!

From the discreetly sure specialist whose guidance we depend on, to the appealling certainty of a rousing speaker, fearless individuals have characteristics that everybody appreciates.

Fearlessness is critical in pretty much every part of our lives, yet such a large number of individuals battle to discover it. Unfortunately, this can be an endless loop: individuals who need fearlessness can think that its hard to get fruitful.

Snap here to see a transcript of this video.

All things considered, the vast majority are hesitant to back an undertaking that is being pitched by somebody who was anxious, bumbling, and excessively sorry.

Then again, you may be convinced by somebody who talks plainly, who holds their head high, who answers questions without a doubt, and who promptly concedes when the person in question doesn't know something.

Certain individuals rouse trust in others: their crowd, their companions, their supervisors, their clients, and their companions. Also, picking up the certainty of others is one of the key manners by which a self-assured individual discovers achievement.

Fortunately self-assurance truly can be learned and based on. Furthermore, regardless of whether you're taking a shot at your own certainty or building the certainty of individuals around you, it's definitely justified even despite the exertion!

How Confident Do You Seem to Others?

Your degree of fearlessness can appear from multiple points of view: your conduct, your non-verbal communication, how you talk, what you state, etc. Take a gander at the accompanying correlations of basic certain conduct with conduct related with low fearlessness. Which contemplations or activities do you perceive in yourself and individuals around you?

Certain Behavior   Behavior Associated With low Self-Confidence

Doing what you accept to be correct, regardless of whether others ridicule or scrutinize you for it.   Governing   your conduct dependent on what others think.
Being happy to go for broke and go the additional mile to accomplish better things.
Staying in your customary range of familiarity, dreading disappointment, thus abstain from going out on a limb.

Conceding your errors, and gaining from them. Working difficult to conceal botches and trusting that you can fix the issue before anybody takes note.

Trusting that others will salute you on your accomplishments. Extolling your own temperances as regularly as conceivable to however many individuals as could be expected under the circumstances.

Tolerating praises charitably. "Much appreciated, I truly buckled down on that outline. I'm satisfied you perceive my efforts."

Dismissing praises casually. "Goodness that outline was nothing truly, anybody could have done it."

As should be obvious from these models, low fearlessness can act naturally damaging, and it regularly shows itself as antagonism. Sure individuals are commonly increasingly positive – they put stock in themselves and their capacities, and they additionally have confidence in making every moment count.

What Is Self-Confidence?

Two principle things add to self-assurance: self-adequacy and confidence.

We increase a feeling of self-adequacy when we see ourselves (as well as other people like ourselves) acing aptitudes and accomplishing objectives that issue in those ability territories. This is the certainty that, on the off chance that we learn and buckle down in a specific territory, we'll succeed; and it's this kind of certainty that leads individuals to acknowledge troublesome demands, and continue even with misfortunes.

Get the Tools You Need to Reach Your Goals!

Get your FREE duplicate of the Life Plan 2020 Toolkit when you join the Mind Tools Club before Midnight PDT, January 09, 2019.

Discover More

This covers with the possibility of confidence , which is a progressively broad sense that we can adapt to what's happening in our lives, and that we reserve an option to be glad. Mostly, this originates from an inclination that the individuals around us favor of us, which we could conceivably have the option to control. Notwithstanding, it additionally originates from the feeling that we are acting highmindedly, that we're skillful at what we do, and that we can contend effectively when we put our brains to it.

A few people accept that self-assurance can be worked with certifications and constructive reasoning . At Mind Tools, we accept that there's a trace of validity in this, yet that it's similarly as imperative to construct self-assurance by defining and accomplishing objectives – along these lines building ability. Without this hidden skill, you don't have fearlessness: you have shallow presumptuousness, with the entirety of the issues, upset and disappointment this brings.

Building Self-Confidence

So how would you manufacture this feeling of adjusted fearlessness, established on a firm valuation for the real world?

The awful news is that there's no convenient solution, or five-minute arrangement.

Fortunately turning out to be progressively sure is promptly reachable, similarly as long as you have the concentration and assurance to bring things through. What's more, what's far superior is that the things you'll do to fabricate your self-assurance will likewise manufacture achievement — all things considered, your certainty will originate from genuine, strong accomplishment. Nobody can remove this from you!

So here are our three stages to self-assurance, for which we'll utilize the analogy of an adventure: getting ready for your voyage; setting out; and quickening towards progress.

Stage 1: Preparing for Your Journey

The initial step includes preparing yourself for your voyage to self-assurance. You have to assess where you are, consider where you need to go, get yourself in the correct mentality for your voyage, and invest in beginning it and remaining with it.

In planning for your adventure, do these five things:

See What You've Already Achieved

Consider your life up until this point, and rundown the ten best things you've accomplished in an "Accomplishment Log." Perhaps you came top in a significant test or test, assumed a key job in a significant group, created the best marketing projections in a period, accomplished something that had a key effect in another person's life, or conveyed a venture that implied a ton for your business.

Put these into an adroitly designed report, which you can take a gander at regularly. And afterward put in no time flat every week getting a charge out of the achievement you've just had!

Consider Your Strengths

Next, utilize a procedure like SWOT Analysis to investigate who and where you are. Taking a gander at your Achievement Log, and pondering your ongoing life, consider what your companions would consider to be your qualities and shortcomings. From these, consider the chances and dangers you face.

Ensure that you appreciate a couple of moments thinking about your qualities!

Consider What's Important to You, and Where You Want to Go

Next, consider the things that are extremely imperative to you, and what you need to accomplish with your life.

Defining and accomplishing objectives is a key piece of this, and genuine certainty originates from this. Objective setting is simply the procedure you use to set targets, and measure your effective hitting of those objectives. See our article on objective setting to discover how to utilize this significant method, or utilize our Life Plan Workbook to thoroughly consider your own objectives in detail (see the "Tip" beneath).

Advise your objective setting with your SWOT Analysis. Set objectives that endeavor your qualities, limit your shortcomings, understand your chances, and control the dangers you face.

What's more, having define the significant objectives throughout your life, distinguish the initial phase in each. Ensure it's a little advance, maybe taking close to an hour to finish!

Start Managing Your Mind

At this stage, you have to begin dealing with your psyche. Figure out how to get and crush the negative self-talk which can devastate your certainty. See our article on sound positive deduction to discover how to do this. Further helpful perusing remembers our article for symbolism – this shows you how to utilize and make solid mental pictures of what you'll feel and experience as you accomplish your significant objectives – there is something in particular about doing this that makes even significant objectives appear to be attainable!

And afterward Commit Yourself to Success!

The last piece of getting ready for the adventure is to make an obvious and unequivocal guarantee to yourself that you are totally dedicated to your voyage, and that you will do all in your capacity to accomplish it.

Stage 2: Setting Out

This is the place you start, gradually, moving towards your objective. By doing the correct things, and beginning with little, simple successes, you'll put yourself on the way to progress – and start assembling the self-assurance that accompanies this.

Fabricate the Knowledge You Need to Succeed

Taking a gander at your objectives, distinguish the aptitudes you'll have to accomplish them. And afterward take a gander at how you can gain these abilities certainly and well. Don't simply acknowledge a crude, sufficiently great arrangement — search for an answer, a program or a course that completely prepares you to accomplish what you need to accomplish and, in a perfect world, gives you a declaration or capability you can be pleased with.

Concentrate on the Basics

At the point when you're beginning, don't attempt to do anything astute or expand.

Furthermore, don't go after flawlessness —
simply appreciate doing basic things
effectively and well.

Set Small Goals, and Achieve Them

Beginning with the little objectives you
distinguished in stage 1, start setting them,
accomplishing them, and commending that
accomplishment. Try not to make objectives
especially testing at this stage, simply start
accomplishing them and commending them.
Furthermore, gradually, fire accumulating the
triumphs!

Continue Managing Your Mind

Remain over that positive reasoning, continue
celebrating and getting a charge out of

accomplishment, and keep those psychological pictures solid. You can likewise utilize a strategy like Treasure Mapping to make your perceptions significantly more grounded!

What's more, on the opposite side, figure out how to deal with disappointment. Acknowledge that slip-ups happen when you're taking a stab at something new. Truth be told, in the event that you start regarding botches as learning encounters, you can (nearly) begin to see them in a positive light. All things considered, let's not forget about the colloquialism "on the off chance that it doesn't slaughter you, it makes you more grounded!"

Stage 3: Accelerating Towards Success

By this stage, you'll feel your self-assurance building. You'll have finished a portion of the courses you began in stage 2, and you'll have a lot of achievement to celebrate!

This is simply an opportunity to begin extending. Make the objectives somewhat greater, and the difficulties somewhat harder. Increment the size of your dedication. Also, expand the abilities you've demonstrated into new, however firmly related fields.

Tip 1:

Keep yourself grounded – this is the place individuals will in general get presumptuous and over-stretch themselves. Also, ensure you don't begin getting a charge out of shrewdness for the wellbeing of its own...

Tip 2:

On the off chance that you haven't just seen it, utilize our How Self Confident Are You? test to discover how fearless you are, and to recognize explicit techniques for building fearlessness.

What Is Self Confidence?

In the event that you as of now have a general comprehension of what certainty is, at that point you're prepared to become familiar with a quite certain kind of certainty that the vast majority need and love: fearlessness.

Presently, I'm not catching it's meaning to act naturally certain? What's more, where does fearlessness originated from?

These are amazing inquiries to pose, in such a case that you need to manufacture trust in yourself and become an increasingly fearless individual in general, it's essential to initially comprehend what you're attempting to accomplish.

Understanding fearlessness

Self-assurance is a positive sentiment about yourself and your capacities. In this way, in case you're a self-assured individual, it essentially implies that you like what your identity is, and you additionally like your capacity to accomplish things you need to accomplish.

Burrowing somewhat more profound, you can consider fearlessness similar to a nice sentiment about yourself and your capacities that:

Originates from the manner in which you consider yourself and your capacities

Normally makes you more joyful and increasingly fruitful throughout everyday life

Can stay in any circumstance or condition, even without help from others or without material belongings

Snap on any of these characteristics to become familiar with self-assurance.

With these characteristics, fearlessness is something that advantages you in an incredible manner, in light of the fact that in addition to the fact that it is a nice sentiment that normally makes you more joyful and increasingly fruitful, but at the same time it's something that you can create and keep up in any circumstance or situation.

This is on the grounds that it is fearlessness that originates from inside you, not certainty that originates from others or things that are outer to you.

Where does fearlessness originate from?

Fearlessness originates from your capacities. Thus, you can consider self-assurance as self canfidence, since it originates from things you can do in any circumstance or situation, paying little heed to what others need you to do.

All the more explicitly, fearlessness originates from three ground-breaking capacities that you, similar to each other person, has:

Your capacity to contemplate yourself and your capabilties (instead of adversely)

Your capacity to be sure that you are somebody of positive esteem and have ground-breaking abilities (paying little mind to whether others question this or can't help contradicting you)

Your capacity to keep contemplating yourself and your abilities, in any circumstance or situation, regardless

Having these three ground-breaking capacities makes it workable for you to be extremely self-assured; creating and utilizing these three capacities is the thing that really makes you fearless.

In this way, in the event that you need to turn into an increasingly fearless individual, it's initial a matter of perceiving that you as of now have every one of the capacities that it takes to turn out to be progressively self-assured, and afterward creating and utilizing those capacities to make more noteworthy trust in yourself.

Habitually posed inquiries about self-assurance

Snap on each question to find out additional.

What is genuine self-assurance?

What is a case of fearlessness?

What is low fearlessness?

What is simply the key certainty?

Become familiar with self-assurance

As of now, you have realized what fearlessness is, and how you as of now have all that it takes to create more noteworthy trust in yourself. This is an important accomplishment all by itself, since this information opens the entryway for you to turn into a significantly more certain individual.

The following stage, for you, is to get familiar with the significance and advantages of fearlessness, and why it's to your greatest advantage to act naturally certain, paying little respect to whether others need you to turn out to be increasingly sure or not.

CHAPTER 3
Should there be self confidence for women?

Why Every Woman Needs To Build Self-Confidence

Why building fearlessness is basic for each lady who needs to have a sound relationship and carry on with a blissful life? In this article, you'll become familiar with the genuine reasons why it's significant for each lady to manufacture fearlessness in themselves.

Fearlessness enables you to understand yourself from with an improved point of view.

It is extremely fitting for each woman to believe in themselves. Fearlessness is something that originates from inside thinking about how you hold yourself or how individuals see you.

It makes you love yourselves. You have faith in your idea, your capacities what not. You believe you are only the best form of yourself, which is a great inclination.

Furthermore, it ought not be mistaken for haughtiness. Here are a couple of reasons why you have to improve or chip away at your fearlessness.

It expands your self-esteem:

at the point when you have fearlessness, you

start to welcome yourself and all that you can do and furthermore place your self in a high position.

With self-assurance, you have made an undetectable security ball around yourself. Individuals will regard you when conversing with you due to how you had put yourself.

You discover that you don't simply agree to anything less that comes your direction, since you definitely know your value. Also, it will assist you with finding the perfect individual and fabricate a sound and enduring association with the one you merit.

It enables you to go to bat for yourself:

With fearlessness, you can go to bat for

yourself in each circumstance. Furthermore, you will have the option to represent yourself. Without certainty, individuals may treat you the manner in which they need to, some of the time obnoxiously. With high self-assurance, the only thing that is in any way important is the means by which you see yourself.

You can remain above dread, going from dread of the obscure or dread of what individuals may state about you. Additionally, you can deal with any circumstance that the vast majority avoid.

It likewise enables you to control your feelings and furthermore realize how to carry on mindfully. You can likewise impact what individuals think and how they act.

Individuals will admire you:

With fearlessness, you can turn into individuals' good example. This is on the grounds that individuals will like you and furthermore need to talk and connect themselves with you.

You begin to ponder everything, you accept that nothing is incomprehensible.

It likewise has a method for making you clear. You will end up being the lady for her words.

At the point when you have high self-assurance, you'll center more around self esteem and confidence. What's more, you will have a superior comprehension of yourself and ready to recognize your shortcoming reasonably.

You stand a superior possibility of doing great for your profession, your relationship and your life.

It will keep your accomplice keen on you:

Self-assurance is one of the key privileged insights to keep your accomplice intrigued by you. At the point when you have high self-assurance, you'll become exceptionally appealing. You recognize what you need throughout everyday life and in your relationship, and you will take activities to get it going. This makes you free and alluring, and men acknowledge ladies who have those characteristics. Understand more in the event that you need more tips on the best way to help your trust in your relationship.

End

To put it plainly, fearlessness enables you to vanquish the world. It will assist you with accomplishing beyond what you can envision.

Notwithstanding, self-assurance ought not be mistaken for carelessness which isn't fitting. At the point when you expand on your self-assurance, you become an individual liberated from stresses, stress, tension and then some...

When you have built up fearlessness, you'll see that you become a more joyful individual and life gets charming. In the event that you don't have fearlessness, attempt to take a shot at yourself, it may very well be the start of enormity and joy.

The Self-Confidence Formula for Women

We don't enter the world with it. Nobody has it constantly. Discussing it won't assist you with picking up it. I'm alluding to self-assurance. We ladies have specific trouble creating self-assurance. We instinctually center around everybody except ourselves. So setting aside the effort for self-improvement doesn't fall into place easily for us. Young ladies frequently are urged to be aloof, and not very brave or sure. All things considered, we would prefer not to undermine each one of those folks out there!

We turn on the TV or read the paper, and are shelled by instances of ladies with extraordinary self-assurance. They have a sort of chutzpah that we can't marshal. Jackie Joyner-Kersee, Sandra Day O'Connor and Madame Curie are nevertheless a couple of models.

So how do these ladies make the confidence in self required to push the breaking points of their capacities? How would they keep on trying, even at the danger of open disappointment and embarrassment? In the event that you asked them, their recipe for self-assurance would almost certainly incorporate the accompanying fixings:

Assume liability for yourself. This is the first and most significant fixing in the fearlessness recipe. You, and no one but you, can make new things occur in your life. In the event that you trust that luck will give you favorable luck, or with expanded certainty, you'll be holding up quite a while. Understand that the way toward self-assurance is one that you should travel — nobody else can do it for you.

Start to explore different avenues regarding life. Have a go at something new. Go out to supper alone. Take a class in a new branch of knowledge. Show yourself how to fix a toaster. Testing your capacities at new undertakings is a brilliant method to discover that you can depend on yourself.

Build up an activity plan and actualize it. Select one territory for individual or expert advancement. Decide the move steps you will make to arrive. Put these means on a course of events. Presently execute each progression as indicated by plan — no reasons. Each little advance you take will be an incredible lift to your certainty!

Stick with it. At the point when you take on another test, stay with it. Fearlessness doesn't originate from every thing you endeavor. In the event that it did, one bombed exertion would expedite you back to zero the certainty scale. Genuine certainty creates from an expanding conviction that you can depend on yourself to make a move and finish, regardless of what the outcome.

Act "as though." If you put off making a move until you have certainty, you'll never do it. In the field of brain research we have come to comprehend that by changing our conduct, we can change our emotions. So on the off chance that you make a move, and do as such with a similarity to outward certainty, the internal, genuine sentiment of certainty, will pursue.

Discover a coach. Do you know somebody who is sure and keeps on going out on a limb after another? Watch how they do this. Assemble up the fortitude to approach them to meet you for espresso. Discover how they do what they do, and approach them for criticism about your activity plan and usage. Most certain individuals are glad to help. They recall the fortitude and exertion it's taken them to get where they are today.

Indeed, the fact of the matter is "out of the pack." No more reasons. Not any more insightful murmurs, as you consider that effective tumbler you met, or the lady you read about who came back to therapeutic school in her 60s. Directly here, at this moment, you have the equation to build up your own certainty. So head for the research facility and start making, including each fixing in turn.

The Confidence Gap In Men And Women: Why It Matters And How To Overcome It

In December of 1920, Amelia Earhart paid to go on her first plane ride. The experience kept going just ten minutes, however it altered an amazing course: Amelia was resolved to be a pilot. It didn't make a difference to her that there were just a couple of ladies in the field of avionics. Through difficult work and testing conditions, she built up her aptitudes. While other female pilots dreaded the long voyage over the Transatlantic, Amelia's gutsy assurance drove her to be first lady to fly it solo. The certainty she had was probably the best quality and drove her to establish numerous precedents.

Amelia Earhart was not by any means the only profoundly capable female pilot during that time ever. In spite of the fact that she was talented, I don't accept that is the thing that made her be so fruitful. Or maybe it was her certainty, her readiness to pursue the inconceivable, and her conviction that she could do it. At Zenger Folkman we've seen that certainty demonstrates as similarly as significant as capability since it prompts activity, consideration, and strength—all characteristics exemplified during Amelia's transoceanic flight.

Amelia Earhart's achievements were particularly significant at the time, in view of her accomplishments in what had been a male space. Pilots were almost all men. Sexual orientation contrasts in certainty are very emotional. An examination done at Cornell University found that men overestimate their capacities and execution, while ladies think little of both. Truth be told, their real execution doesn't vary in quality or amount.

Today In: Leadership

This female certainty challenge was additionally depicted as the "faker disorder" by Pauline Claunce and Suzanne Imes. Ladies much of the time express that they don't feel they merit their activity and are "shams" who could be discovered at any minute. They found that ladies stress increasingly over being despised, seeming ugly, surpassing others, or catching an excessive amount of eye.

Men are not absolve from questioning themselves—however they don't let their questions stop them as regularly as ladies do. A Hewlett Packard inward report found that men go after a position or advancement when they meet just 60% of the capabilities, yet ladies apply just on the off chance that they meet 100% of them. What destined them was not their real capacity, but instead the choice not to attempt.

Advanced

Deloitte BRANDVOICE

| Paid Program

Ensuring Our Future: Moving From Talk To Action On The Sustainable Development Goals

DBS Private Bank BRANDVOICE

| Paid Program

A Customized Approach Is Key In Wealth Management Today

Urban Nation BRANDVOICE

| Paid Program

Arrive at Higher's Top 5 Moments Of 2019

Zenger Folkman's examination shows that as ladies' experience increments after some time, so does their certainty. The chart underneath shows that ladies' certainty builds more with age than men's. Be that as it may, consider the numerous open doors lost in early years in light of dread and absence of certainty.

uncaptioned

Building fearlessness

I wish there were conclusive strides to fabricate fearlessness and confidence, yet I don't think they exist. Nonetheless, there are various things you can do that seem, by all accounts, to be identified with more elevated levels of certainty and confidence.

Outlook: It has been said that fearlessness is your opinion of yourself, and confidence is the thing that you think others consider you. To fabricate fearlessness:

Concentrate on the qualities you have and your accomplishments, instead of what you don't progress admirably. Gatekeeper cautiously against negative self-talk.

Emanate confidence and general bliss. They bring life and essentialness into discussions. Your outward conduct changes your inward emotions.

Individuals are pulled in to the individuals who are seen as "warm" and avoid the individuals who are seen as "chilly." The self-assured individual is normally depicted as being warm. Dress and prepping: These are quick and unmistakable sign to others about how you feel about yourself. Past that, they have been appeared to have any kind of effect by they way somebody feels about themselves. Primary concern, individuals feel progressively certain when they realize they look decent.

Stance: Your stance strongly affects what you're feeling inside.

Stand tall. Research has demonstrated that when somebody stands tall in a place of solidarity, their inward sentiments start to change.

Look at others. This passes on enthusiasm for other people and trust in yourself.

Outward appearances impart significant messages and should be steady with words being said. Some gauge that at any rate 80% of correspondence comes non-verbally, and outward appearance passes on a lot of data.

By and large way: How you carry on will transmit a sentiment of certainty to other people. Certain individuals:

Walk energetically, passing on that they have some place imperative to go and something critical to do.

Snicker with others and cause them to giggle. This doesn't really originate from making quips, however as a rule originates from lovely chat with respect to themes of shared intrigue.

Make some noise in gatherings. They don't sit unobtrusively through discourses, however are a functioning member.

Associate with numerous individuals when placed into an enormous assembling as opposed to binding themselves to long discussions with a few for a whole night.

Start contact with others, not trusting that others will come to them. Certain individuals stretch out themselves to an a lot bigger number of individuals than their less-sure partners.

Discourse: What you state and how you state it transmits a lot about your degree of certainty. It likewise shapes how you feel about yourself. Certain individuals:
Undertaking their voice, making them effectively heard and comprehended.

Differ the pitch and tone of their voice. They make their discussion intriguing by staying away from monotones and infusing assortment.

Delay for accentuation—they are not scared of snapshots of quietness. Not filling each delay further passes on close to home sentiments of self-esteem and certainty. At times these stops are utilized to accumulate time to think, take a full breath, or pull together a discourse.

Utilize a rich jargon, empowering them to be striking and pre They keep on building up a solid jargon, not to dazzle, yet to assist thoughts with becoming animated. Bright, instinctive words make their correspondence paramount.

They keep away from "non-words, for example, "er," "umm," and filler-expressions, for example, "you know."

Correspondence rehearses: Confident people use correspondence rehearses that pass on conviction with others while additionally making them feel progressively certain inside themselves. For instance, they:

Much of the time pose inquiries of others, demonstrating extreme enthusiasm for what others state and in what they are doing.
Use representations, models, and stories generously. Correspondence wakes up with representations that make the conceptual increasingly concrete and hypothetical thoughts effectively comprehended.

Use silliness to make significant focuses.

Certain individuals are regularly bosses of self-deploring humor. Individuals of stature and achievement are the ones generally ready to make jokes about themselves.

Express thoughts consciously, never with pointless showdown. On the off chance that their thoughts contrast from others, this is bound to be communicated as, "I see this somewhat better," or, "Help me to comprehend your explanations behind reasoning... "

Amelia Earhart had the guts and moxie to accept each open door in any event, when she was uncertain on the off chance that she was equipped enough to do it. Nobody knows it all, and the vast majority—male and female— have snapshots of feeling they are fakers attempting to demonstrate their ability and worth. Fortunately for ladies and men, certainty continues expanding after some time.

"Certainty is the stuff that transforms contemplations without hesitation" Richard Petty, Ohio State University

After suddenly removing six years from the workforce to bring up my two little girls, I experienced intense nervousness when I later came back to proficient life. In spite of having kept my abilities ebb and flow by finishing a subsequent degree and exploring and distributing, A World of Difference, I endured an incapacitating certainty hole when I propelled my consultancy in 2012.

To adapt to the uneasiness, I dealt with my work routine cautiously so I had adequate space to deal with my feelings over my remaining burden. However, I realized that working in a condition of dread was not reasonable. To begin with, uneasiness was keeping me from performing at my best. Second, enthusiastic and physical depletion was constraining the quantity of assignments I could take on. Third, my wellbeing was enduring. I either needed to surrender or overcome the dread. Subsequent to contributing four years at college and three years inquiring about and composing, A World of Difference, surrendering was impossible. Rather, I examined and explored different avenues regarding various proof based answers for creating self-assurance. Applying those strategies, I had the option to defeat the uneasiness and self-constraining convictions that had been keeping me down.

In this blog, I share the demonstrated methodologies for creating fearlessness that helped me move from 'hare in the headlights' to 'feel the dread and do it at any rate'. I trust by sharing these methods, I can engage other people who are experiencing self-uncertainty to accomplish their maximum capacity.

Strategies FOR DEVELOPING SELF-CONFIDENCE

People with significant levels of certainty have both (a) high self-adequacy and (b) low dread of disappointment. Self-adequacy is one's faith in their capacity to succeed and includes a positive appraisal of one's abilities. Low dread of disappointment is connected to a penchant for venturing outside one's customary range of familiarity. Strategies for creating self-assurance address either self-adequacy, dread of disappointment, or both.

Testing Self-Limiting Beliefs

Ladies, specifically, regularly have various self-restricting convictions that keep them from stepping forward. Young ladies rise up out of pre-adulthood with a poor mental self view, moderately low desires from life and significantly less trust in themselves and their capacities than young men, To gain ground on certainty, we have to challenge negative self-accounts (for example 'I am bad enough/savvy enough/truly enough) and supplant with progressively sympathetic and hopeful self-talk.

There are three stages to testing your self-constraining convictions and overhauling your inward story:

Distinguish your self-constraining convictions. Some of you may be now deliberately mindful of your internal questions and fears. Some of you may need to invest some energy burrowing further to distinguish the considerations that are keeping you away from making a move. A decent method to pinpoint your self-constraining convictions is to screen your enthusiastic triggers. On the off chance that there are specific circumstances that make you feel on edge or apprehensive, set aside some effort to consider what convictions are driving those feelings. Being aware of your inward account through the span of a workday can assist you with articulating your self-constraining convictions. Notice whether and when you make light of your accomplishments or on the off chance that you credit your triumphs to other people or karma. Notice additionally any examinations you make of yourself to other people. Examinations are normally one-sided—we notice the outward accomplishments of others yet neglect to see their interior battles, weaknesses, and restrictions. We center around our very own flaws and neglect to perceive our accomplishments.

Challenge your self-constraining convictions. When you have distinguished your self-restricting convictions – regardless of whether as self-questions, making light of our accomplishments, or adversely contrasting ourselves with others—we should challenge those convictions via looking for proof that repudiates them. Locate the counter-contention to your self-constraining conviction. On the off chance that you locate this difficult to do, take a stab at removing yourself from your self-restricting conviction by envisioning that you are training a companion on the best way to challenge their self-constraining conviction. How might you work them out of that negative self-talk and persuade them generally? At that point apply that counsel to your own circumstance.

Change the account. The third step is to supplant your self-constraining convictions with a progressively discerning, sensible and idealistic story.

Claim Your Achievements

Studies show that ladies tend to credit condition or others for their victories. Men appear to do the inverse, attributing their prosperity to their endeavors and gifts. At the point when you credit your triumphs to factors outside yourself, this undermines certainty.

For what reason do ladies do this? Some contend that ladies may neglect to claim their accomplishments because of a paranoid fear of repudiating ladylike jobs by being seen as indecent, aggressive or bombastic. Since early on, young ladies figure out how to make light of their accomplishments as a method for building affinity with different young ladies.

There are additionally social measurements to owning your accomplishments. For individuals from collectivist societies crosswise over Africa, Asia, and the Middle-East, humility is a significant social worth. While visiting Thailand, I was educated 'the gold stands behind the Buddha'. Individuals from those societies are associated to make light of their individual accomplishments and to credit their victories to other people.

Work on recognizing your capacities by outlining 'feature minutes' over your scholastic, profession and individual life. Consider the inward assets and capacities that upheld every accomplishment and note those recorded as a hard copy. In snapshots of self-question, allude to your graph of accomplishments.

Contain Your Failures

While ladies are less inclined to claim their accomplishments comparative with men, the invert is valid for attributions of disappointments. Though ladies will in general credit inability to their absence of inborn ability or exertion, men will in general accuse disappointment for outer conditions like the trouble of the assignment. Additionally, while men will in general contain an inability to that specific case, ladies tend to react to disappointment in an increasingly worldwide manner questioning the entirety of their capacities and scrutinizing their whole self-esteem. This makes disappointment especially aversive to ladies. On the off chance that a specific occurrence of disappointment is seen as a negative reflection on one's whole capacity or worldwide self-esteem, any circumstance that gives a chance to disappointment can be tremendously threatening to a ladies' self-idea. Contrasted and men, ladies are bound to keep away from circumstances where there is a plausibility of disappointment trying to secure their self-idea and confidence.

Since attribution designs are constant, disturbing worldwide and interior attributions of disappointments expects regard for thought designs after a disappointment or mishap and purposefully testing unhelpful attributions. Calendar time for a purposeful and genuine appraisal of both the outer and inner variables that added to the disappointment. Additionally make certain to adjust negative appraisals of execution by recognizing what functioned admirably.

Recognize Role-Models

Studies affirm the significance of good examples for female certainty and execution. In 2013 researchers asked 149 understudies from a Swiss college (81 ladies, 68 men) to give an enticing political discourse against expanding understudy charges, inside the setting of a computer generated experience program that put them before a group of people of six men and six ladies. For certain members, the back mass of the virtual room included a balancing image of Hillary Clinton. For other people, it indicated a representation of Bill Clinton or Angela Merkel, and for a few, the divider stayed clear. The scientists planned and recorded the discourse, at that point requested that the understudies assess their exhibition. A different gathering of individuals ignorant of the test conditions viewed the discourses and appraised them dependent on familiarity and non-verbal communication. Both the individuals viewing the discourses and those giving them saw longer talks as being progressively positive. When there was no good example in see, men talked longer than ladies. The equivalent remained constant for talking under the shrinking look of Big Bill. Female good examples disposed of the sex hole, however. Ladies gave longer talks and assessed themselves all the more emphatically when they were prepared with pictures of Hillary Clinton and Angela Merkel than when they saw Bill Clinton or weren't prepared in any way. The outside eyewitnesses additionally appraised their discourses higher. The analysts presumed that female good examples can motivate ladies and assist them with adapting to upsetting circumstances that they experience in their professions, for example, open talking. (Study extricate duplicated from Australian Popular Science).

In 2014, Bain discharged the consequences of its examination on working environment certainty and aspiration. The outcomes indicated that ladies leave on professions with exclusive requirements and desires for headway, yet this certainty dissipates drastically as they enter mid-vocation. About portion of all new female representatives seek to top administration in any case, inside five years, just 16 percent still hold that desire; this contrasts and 34 percent of men who start their professions with goals that they will arrive at the top and remain so following at least two years of experience. The checked drop in female yearning is coordinated by a fall in proficient certainty though men experience an a lot littler fall in certainty over a similar period.

Investigating to the causes behind the decrease in proficient certainty and aspiration of ladies, Bain found a 39% decay among new and experienced ladies in feeling that they fit in as far as meeting run of the mill generalizations of progress inside the organization, versus 23% decay for men. Review reactions from experienced ladies demonstrated that the lack of ladies in upper administration to fill in as good examples hampered progress toward sexual orientation equality.

Lady pauses for a minute to make the most of her espresso and the daylight on her face.Earlier this week I took part without precedent for a "women's night out" tennis cooperative occasion in my locale. All through the night, I ended up seeing what number of shouts of "sorry" I continued hearing over every one of the courts.

From my work in driving confidence workshops, I realize numerous ladies will in general customize botches and over-apologize for even the littlest of mistakes. Along these lines, I thought that it was diverting to observe firsthand what number of conciliatory sentiments were being tossed around during what was at last a laid-back, fun occasion.

I started to ponder: Do men say "sorry" this much when they are playing sports? Do they apologize for each missed shot or bungle? While I don't know without a doubt, I expect that by and large, ladies presumably do this all the more frequently. This isn't intended to generalization, however the truth of the matter is, by and large, ladies appear to battle with the inclination to over-apologize. Also, it likely identifies with confidence.

While taking a gander at look into for my as of late discharged book The Self-Esteem Workbook for Women: 5 Steps to Gaining Confidence and Inner Strength, I went over the aftereffects of an intriguing investigation that discovered ladies do have lower levels of

152

confidence than men and this disparity is watched around the world (Bleidorn, 2016).

As of late, we are finding out increasingly more about the mind and making sense of how neurological variables assume a job in different conditions. Truly, hardly any examinations have taken a gander at the neurological premise of confidence; in any case, a 2014 Dartmouth College study indicated that degrees of confidence are identified with how various areas of the mind interface: People with solid white issue associations from the average prefrontal cortex, the zone managing self-information, to the ventral striatum, the zone managing reward frameworks, exhibited significant levels of confidence over the long haul. A well-working association with significant levels of movement between these two regions related with high confidence at the time. These outcomes recommend that sentiments of self-esteem may originate from neurological associations incorporating data about the self with positive effect and prize.

This depiction may sound confused and profoundly specialized, however the significant point behind this exploration is that associations and combinations in the mind assume a job in confidence. What's more, these associations may work diversely for people.

It's fascinating to think about how science adds to the confidence contrasts we observer between sexes, yet I'm not catching this' meaning for ladies? Since ladies have all the earmarks of being inclined to bring down degrees of confidence, it's everything the more significant for ladies to effectively find a way to manufacture confidence. How would we do this?

Tragically, the apparatuses important to help fabricate confidence aren't educated in adolescence or in most educational systems; regularly, they are things people adapt just when they end up battling with temperament or relationship issues that cause them to look for help. However, I accept everybody, particularly ladies, merits fearlessness and can profit by building up an attention to the stuff to discover internal quality. Since confidence impacts each everyday issue—vocation, connections, child rearing, enthusiastic wellbeing, and by and large prosperity—it's crucial to increase a superior comprehension of how you can effectively assemble and keep up a sound feeling of self-esteem.

Since ladies seem, by all accounts, to be inclined to bring down degrees of confidence, it's everything the more significant for ladies to effectively find a way to fabricate confidence.

In The Self-Esteem Workbook for Women, I give five stages activities and contextual analyses to manage ladies in improving their confidence. Laid out underneath is a review.

For a more profound investigate the five stages, I urge you to look at the exercise manual, where you can move however each progression on an individual level and at your very own pace.

1. Know Yourself

Building confidence initially includes knowing who you are: distinguishing what you like, comprehending what you truly desire, and building up an attention to how your past encounters have formed the individual you are today. It requires focusing on how you treat yourself and building up a consciousness of the inward messages you ponder.

2. Care for Yourself

Creating solid confidence likewise incorporates perceiving how incredible your inner voice is and figuring out how to revamp your cerebrum by growing progressively viable reasoning examples. It includes going about as your own team promoter and being careful that things, for example, diet, exercise, rest, and setting practical desires all assume a job by they way you feel about yourself. Past the essentials, thinking about yourself implies guaranteeing you invest significant time to support your soul by doing things you appreciate.

3. Regard Yourself

Regarding yourself is essential to keeping up solid confidence. It includes surveying and maintaining your qualities without yielding your prosperity to satisfy others. It's tied in with creating trust in yourself and learning abilities to turn out to be progressively decisive.

4. Acknowledge Yourself

Cultivating sound confidence includes recognizing your breaking points and flaws, tolerating slip-ups, and figuring out how to all the more successfully manage reactions. It requires knowing your limit for pressure, creating self-empathy, and excusing yourself for shortcomings or stumbles.

5. Love Yourself

To really show confidence, you should trust in your value and care about your future. Cherishing yourself implies regarding yourself just as you treat companions and friends and family. Improving limits seeing someone. It likewise involves commending your qualities and figuring out how to acknowledge praises. This page contains at any rate one offshoot connect for the Amazon Services LLC Associates Program, which implies GoodTherapy.org gets money related remuneration on the off chance that you make a buy utilizing an Amazon interface.

These means may sound excessively shortsighted; on the other hand, they may sound overpowering. Yet, building solid confidence is conceivable. It requires you to effectively turn internal and build up a more prominent feeling of mindfulness. With committed exertion, centered consideration, and an eagerness to incorporate new devices, you can construct confidence and experience a more noteworthy degree of certainty. Doing so will push you to at last accomplish an all the more remunerating life.

Ladies and the Negativity Receptor

Can any anyone explain why ladies get on the smallest slur and never hear the great stuff? Reactions are put away always; praises dissipate quickly.

My goddaughter, visiting from school, is spread on my bed while we authorize one of our normal customs: I scrutinize my wardrobe, offering her the garments I never again wear. "Take this, I don't have the legs for short skirts," I state, or "These jeans make me look hippy." She respects me with curious beguilement, recommending that I have body dysmorphic scatter—that I'm one of those individuals distracted with minor, and regularly fanciful, blemishes in physical highlights. At any rate, she demands, I need new glasses.

Also, we're not talking negligible physical instability. At the point when I meet a book editorial manager about a potential distributing contract, I fuss about my capacities, limiting a flourishing vocation and a notoriety on favorable terms of over 20 years. In the event that visitors are wanting supper, I stress that my home won't be satisfying, that my brownies won't justify the caloric consumption, that the discussion won't be adequately shining. Some way or another I figure out how to explore life genuinely well, to acquire a living and have connections, to stroll without weaving and bite without spitting. Yet, as I viewed the film Pretty Woman as of late, it struck me that a lot of us have a similar self-question that crashed the Julia Roberts character. There's where she's telling the affluent specialist played by Richard Gere that no one ever plans to be a hooker, that she fell into this profession since she didn't appreciate herself. Gere sees that she's an extraordinary individual with a great deal of potential and capacities. Also, she answers, "The awful stuff is simpler to accept."

Why it that a few people, the Donald Trumps of the world, appear to accept simply the best about themselves, while others—maybe particularly ladies, maybe particularly young ladies—seize on the most self-basic musings they can concoct? "It turns out there's a zone of your mind that is doled out the errand of negative reasoning," says Louann Brizendine, MD, a neuropsychiatrist at the University of California, San Francisco, and the creator of The Female Brain. "It's critical. It says 'I'm excessively fat' or 'I'm excessively old.' It's an indicator of each social connection you have. It goes on red ready when the criticism you're getting from others isn't working out positively." This killjoy some portion of the mind is the front cingulate cortex. In ladies, it's really bigger and increasingly compelling, just like the cerebrum hardware for watching feelings in others. "The explanation we think females have progressively enthusiastic affectability," says Brizendine, "is that we've been worked to be promptly receptive to the necessities of a nonverbal baby. That can be both something to be thankful for and an awful thing."

The hormonal floods in the female cerebrum—what Brizendine portrays as the rising tide of estrogen and progesterone—make a lady increasingly touchy to enthusiastic subtlety, for example, dissatisfaction or dismissal. The manner in which you translate criticism from others can rely upon where you are in your cycle. "A few days the input will fortify your fearlessness," says Brizendine, "and different days it will demolish you." Her choice to make this hormone cycle in the female cerebrum the focal point of her examination was made in therapeutic school, when she was working with youths at Yale–New Haven Hospital. "How teenager young ladies come to accept awful stuff about themselves truly enamored me," she says. "There is something in particular about the menstrual cycle that places your passionate self in an awful light at any rate a couple of days consistently. Around 90 percent of ladies feel some sort of expanded emotionality two to four days before their period begins, where they're crying over canine nourishment plugs. I needed to get a message to young ladies who are descending some elusive slant and get a security net under them."

Researchers are practically in understanding that at any rate half of your character originates from your genetic supply—it's a piece of the personality card you're given during childbirth. Educational encounters help to shape the other half. On the off chance that you procure some thought regarding yourself—maybe you're known as the issue kid in a study hall or the good-for-nothing in a family—that thought will affect your cerebrum hardware and get incorporated with how you consider yourself. "Our human minds love to arrange and name—'the truly one' or 'the reliable one' or 'the keen one,'" says Brizendine. "At that point you become used to the mark and frequently re-make that character since it feels natural. It can mean a wide range of treats yet in addition a wide range of weights."

The main time I go into Old Navy is the point at which I need an adolescent suitable blessing. (I by and large have a standard: If I can't stand the store's music, I'm too old to even consider wearing the store's garments.) But as of late I was lured into the changing area by the draw of cool modest stuff and found a virtual petri dish of young defenselessness about accepting the terrible stuff—I listened in on one mournful "Does this make me look fat?" after another. "One of the significant undertakings of youth is, 'Who are you?'" says Jessica Henderson Daniel, PhD, partner teacher of brain science at Harvard Medical School. "Having a place and finding your specialty as far as resources and liabilities is shaded by what others see—since you don't live in an air pocket. As a rule, young ladies don't look like what they figure they ought to resemble." There is a basic lucky opening in early youth when it is conceivable to imbue a young lady with a feeling of self-esteem that did not depend on the size of her bosoms or the shine of her hair, says Daniel. "Individuals for the most part miss the mark regarding the media perfect, which is the reason I advocate helping adolescents get ready for youth in their rudimentary years, developing their aptitudes so they have evidence that they are in excess of a picture. Adolescents who have pride in achievement are more tied down."

An investigation at the University of Texas how effectively self-perception is undermined: A gathering of juvenile young ladies were in a stay with an alluring lady who griped about how fat she was (the suggestion being that anyone who was heavier than she would truly have something to whine about). There was a prompt effect on the self-perception of the young ladies, despite the fact that the experience was brief and the lady was an outsider. "Up to 50 percent of immature young ladies have self-perception concerns," says Eric Stice, PhD, lead specialist on that review. "Up to 70 percent of young ladies state they would take a pill to shed five pounds; with guys, it's perhaps 15 percent. Also, pubescence pushes youngsters toward the perfect male self-perception, solid and built, yet moves young ladies from the perfect female self-perception, lean without any hips. It's extremely dismal that immature young ladies take a gander at enhanced with Photoshop pictures in the media that aren't even genuine. They're executing themselves for something that isn't genuine."

I had marvelous guardians and other people who reliably let me realize I was savvy, lovely, and esteemed. Be that as it may, for certain individuals, the foundations of accepting the terrible stuff as grown-ups may lie with guardians who don't show confidence in a youngster's capacities, and no different grown-ups are around to give light. "There's a pleasant collection of proof demonstrating that children with at any rate one strong grown-up who checks these messages can discover roads for communicating the positive sides of themselves," says Susan Nolen-Hoeksema, PhD, an educator of brain research at Yale and the creator of Women Who Think Too Much. Parental sadness is promptly transmitted to kids, as well. "The guardians see the world in negative terms and present this view to their kids," says Nolen-Hoeksema. "They're excessively critical and bad tempered toward their children. They would prefer not to be, yet it's a piece of their issue. Those children have a genuine inclination to receive self-basic reasoning. It will in general be sustained over each part of a kid's life, particularly in a little network, where you remain in a similar school locale, and your siblings and sisters are in a similar region, and the instructors know your folks. You remain 'the chunky young lady' or 'the skanky young lady.' It's extremely difficult to shake off."

One explanation it's difficult to shake off is the thing that clinicians call the drive for self-check—to have others mirror the convictions we hold about ourselves. The vast majority are exceptionally energetic to accept the best of themselves, and unobtrusively or not really, they search for input from others to affirm these nice sentiments. In any case, somebody who's discouraged will go out and look for negative criticism, confirming her own musings. In a recent report by Thomas E. Joiner, PhD, a brain science educator at Florida State University, the self-confirmation rationale was amazing to such an extent that it abrogated the agony of negative conclusions. What's more, a recent report coauthored by Joiner's partner brain science educator Roy F. Baumeister, PhD, affirmed that "terrible is more grounded than great": Bad input, awful child rearing, and awful encounters are considerably more dominant than great ones. Individuals recall the awful more clearly, process it all the more effectively, and give more consideration to it. Terrible impressions or generalizations structure all the more rapidly, and negative emotions produce longer-enduring impacts. So my mind fools me into recollecting all the more strikingly the infrequent cooking calamity (a snapshot of quiet now for the heavy spinach gnocchi I once foisted on blameless visitors) than the dominance of tasty nourishment I've cooked. Or on the other hand the hopeless time of my life when I was harmed, couldn't work out, and increased 10 pounds rather than a mind-blowing remainder when I've fit into thin pants.

Normally, the friend bunch has incredible control over what you accept about yourself. "On the off chance that different children are calling you names and don't need you on their groups, you get it with lightning speed," says

Nolen-Hoeksema. I was reliably the last one picked for volleyball, and right up 'til today I see myself as an individual with zero athletic ability.

At the point when you hear 'certain lady' a great many people will naturally have the picture of somebody they reverberate inside their brain. This individual is effectively seen, they depict achievement and they transmit joy. They are your ideal image of 'certainty'.

In any case, what is it about these individuals that makes them certain? Similarly as with most attributes, there are sure propensities for certain ladies that you can apply to your life to support your certainty and thusly increment the bliss you have inside yourself.

Play Video

Proceeding with our 11 Habits arrangement, here are the 11 Habits of a Confident Woman. You don't have to have them all to be certain, yet you would be unable to locate a sure lady who didn't have some of these without a doubt.

Fearlessness isn't something you simply 'have'. It's something that takes work to accomplish and afterward it's something you have to make a propensity. Here are the best 11 propensities for a sure lady - what number of these propensities do you have?

1 – She Questions The 'Norm'

Infrequently will you locate a certain lady who just takes the path of least resistance, never addressing what she is told, what the 'standard' is and simply being amazingly normal.

I'm not discussing the ladies who contend each point, or even the ladies who discover zen in enabling life to unfurl in the 'stream' – yet more so the ones that never question 'why'.

For what reason would you say you are doing what you're doing? Is it since that is the manner in which it's constantly been finished?
Is there a superior way?

She isn't hesitant to state 'really, no that doesn't work for me, how about we attempt it along these lines'. What's more, considerably further to that, she isn't reluctant to state 'really that didn't work, how about we have a go at something else once more'.

Self-assurance isn't something you simply 'have'. It's something that takes work to accomplish and afterward it's something you have to make a propensity. Here are the best 11 propensities for a certain lady - what number of these propensities do you have?

2 – She Reserves The Word 'Yes' For When She Really Means It

We as a whole realize that one individual (perhaps it's even you) that says yes to everything!! She wouldn't like to allow anybody to down and she wouldn't like to frustrate anybody. Be that as it may, in doing as such, she winds up continually accomplishing for other people and not for herself.

Sound well-known?

'No' is a troublesome word for many individuals to state. That is on the grounds that it is immediate and conclusive. A 'no' is a conclusion of a discussion and is an incredible word that can hurt when utilized erroneously.

A certain lady realizes that idiom 'no' to others frequently implies she is stating 'yes' to herself.

Furthermore, when you state 'yes' to other people, you need to mean it that way. Since it for the most part implies you'll be quitting any trace of something for yourself (time, vitality) and when you do say indeed, you don't half-arse it and you would not joke about this. That is the reason a 'yes' from a certain lady implies to such an extent.

Fearlessness isn't something you simply 'have'. It's something that takes work to accomplish and afterward it's something you have to make a propensity. Here are the main

11 propensities for a sure lady - what number of these propensities do you have?

3 – She Uses Positive Words In Her Conversations

A business guide of mine once disclosed to me how significant our words are. His model was to do with basic words we use in our ordinary discussions.

As opposed to stating 'remember' he disclosed to state 'please recall. We are unmistakably bound to react to positive words than negative ones.

A certain lady utilizes positive words in her discussions to develop herself as well as other people. She doesn't need to take care of others down for her to like herself.

A discussion with a sure lady will leave you feeling motivated.

Understand This: 5 Labels We Need To Stop Giving Women

Self-assurance isn't something you simply 'have'. It's something that takes work to accomplish and afterward it's something you have to make a propensity. Here are the main 11 propensities for a sure lady - what number of these propensities do you have?

4 – She Has Clear Goals And Action Plans To Achieve Them

A sure lady gets that while objectives are significant, they don't mean anything except if you have an activity plan set up to accomplish them.

It's fine and dandy to stay here and state 'I will likely gain enough cash so I can leave my place of employment', and that is wonderful. Be that as it may, except if you have an arrangement set up concerning how you will accomplish it, your objective is just a fantasy.

Objectives, activity plans and following are on the whole territories a sure lady comprehends and utilizes well.

Utilize our Free Mini Life Planner to assist you with making and track your objectives:

Download Our FREE MiniLife Planner

Sort out and Simplify your existence with the FREE Mini Life Planner. With 10 pages intended to assist you with taking control and life a glad, composed life.

Name

Email

SEND IT TO ME

SPAM sucks and we could never send it to you. See our Privacy Policy for more subtleties.

5 – She Knows That Confidence Is Far More Than Appearance, But Knows The Benefit Of Her 'Capacity Outfit'

Everybody has in any event one outfit or one thing of dress that causes them to feel certain, ground-breaking and like they could take on the world. Their Power Outfit.

And keeping in mind that we realize that certainty is undeniably more than appearance, we additionally comprehend that any little lift in certainty we can get, regardless of whether it originates from a flawlessly some jeans and executioner heels, is justified, despite all the trouble.

Understand This: 5 Ways To Boost Your Self Confidence

Self-assurance isn't something you simply 'have'. It's something that takes work to accomplish and afterward it's something you have to make a propensity. Here are the main 11 propensities for a certain lady - what number of these propensities do you have?

6 – She Displays Confident Body Language

Picture Wonder Woman... just with more garments on and less wind machine blowing her hair around.

Truly however, there is a ton of brain research behind the advantages of the power present and a sure lady utilizes this to further her potential benefit. In any event, when she's not feeling too sure that day, she realizes that she can counterfeit it until she makes it with a power present.

Furthermore, you will seldom observe her drooped over or cringing in a group. A certain lady stands tall, looks at individuals without flinching when she is conversing with them and grins, since she puts stock in herself.

Fearlessness isn't something you simply 'have'. It's something that takes work to accomplish and afterward it's something you have to make a propensity. Here are the best 11 propensities for a certain lady - what number of these propensities do you have?

7 – She Has A Good Understanding Of Her Own Personality – Including Her Strengths And Weaknesses

Understanding your very own character can be critical to your prosperity. A sure lady knows her qualities and shortcomings and realizes how to utilize them furthering her potential benefit.

Maybe she can pass on her message best when talking, however battles with thinking of her contemplations down. Straightforward fix – record what you need to state and have a transcriber work it out for you.

Maybe she realizes she is undeniably increasingly tolerant at around 10am when she has had the opportunity to have her espresso, react to messages and work out her assignment list for the afternoon. Fabulous — she knows not to book any gatherings until after that time.

Taking a character test (like this one) can enable you to turn out to be considerably increasingly sure about what your identity is, and figure out how to be additionally tolerating of your shortcomings.

Fearlessness isn't something you simply 'have'. It's something that takes work to accomplish and afterward it's something you have to make a propensity. Here are the best 11 propensities for a sure lady - what number of these propensities do you have?

8 – She Creates Her Own Success Without Feeling The Need To Tear Others Down

You will never hear a sure lady state 'well I did that superior to you' since she realizes that her own prosperity has nothing to do with others disappointments.

Her victories are her own, she endeavors to accomplish them and comprehends that others triumphs are the equivalent.

Correlation isn't a snare she falls into (time and again) and she is glad to assist somebody with praising their own prosperity, regardless of whether she hasn't accomplished hers at this time.

Fearlessness isn't something you simply 'have'. It's something that takes work to accomplish and afterward it's something you have to make a propensity. Here are the main 11 propensities for a sure lady - what number of these propensities do you have?

9 – She Focuses On The Positive And Leaves Negative Behaviors (And People) Behind

Being around a sure lady resembles having a monstrous infusion of energy tossed into your day. She lacks the capacity to deal with the Negative Nellies of the world and expels them from her life.

She has this awesome capacity to see the positive in any circumstance and leaves you feeling enlivened.

Sure she has her terrible days everybody does. Furthermore, she isn't 100% positive constantly, in light of the fact that that is simply unimaginable. Be that as it may, she endeavors to see the constructive on the planet and encircle herself with constructive individuals and positive things.

A Lack of Confidence Isn't What's Holding Back Working Women

Ladies are reluctant to talk up their achievements since they are frequently punished when they do.

This much we know: There's a wide and difficult sexual orientation hole, both as far as pay and authority openings. What despite everything we can't make sense of are the causes. Some contend that unbendable work environments are at fault. Others point to chauvinist social standards and even through and through segregation.

While the fact of the matter is most likely a blend of every one of these components, and then some, another hypothesis has made progress as of late. Now and then alluded to as the "certainty hole," the hypothesis holds that ladies feel less sure than men in their own capacities, and in a corporate world that prizes horn tooters more than the unassuming, ladies' inclination to abstain from advancing themselves and their achievements implies they're disregarded for enormous undertakings, influential positions, and increases in salary. The arrangement, ladies are told, is straightforward: Go forward with the certainty of a man, and that corner office will be yours. On the off chance that offers of books like Lean In and The Confidence Code are any sign, numerous ladies have accepted this translation with barely a second thought.

How adolescence murders young ladies' certainty

There's only one issue: There's a solid collection of research proposing that ladies feel similarly as certain about their capacities and authority aptitudes as their male companions. The certainty hole is by all accounts a great instance of mixing up the indication—ladies' clear failure to advance themselves—for the reason. "Ladies do appear to toot their horns not exactly their male associates," says Hannah Riley Bowles, a senior instructor in open strategy at the Harvard Kennedy School who examines ladies' administration. "The issue is the point at which you stop there and state, 'Alright, well, ladies simply should be progressively similar to men.' The tale of why ladies are more unobtrusive than men is substantially more entangled than that."

MORE STORIES

How Puberty Kills Girls' Confidence

CLAIRE SHIPMAN KATTY KAY JILLELLYN RILEY

The Confidence Gap

KATTY KAY CLAIRE SHIPMAN

What Gender Pay-Gap Statistics Aren't Capturing

BOURREE LAM

Together, two new bits of research are distinguishing why it's so difficult for ladies to gloat about their achievements. The main examination, directed by analysts at three European business colleges, affirms what many working ladies instinctually know: While they may be advised certainty is the way to proficient achievement, that is once in a while the case practically speaking. Except if ladies can temper their emphaticness with all the more characteristically female qualities like sympathy and selflessness, certainty will do little to propel their professions.

Dissecting information from an anonymous worldwide innovation organization, the specialists found that the presence of fearlessness was not similarly compensated for people. "The more certain male designers in our example had all the earmarks of being, the more impact they had in the association," the specialists closed. "Ladies had the option to interpret their self-assured picture into impact just when they likewise showed high prosocial direction, or the inspiration to profit others."

While all that most men appear to require so as to prevail in the working environment is a smidgen of spunk, ladies must figure out how to ace the craft of seeming both certain about themselves and unassuming. A lot of the last mentioned, and ladies' accomplishments get disregarded. A lot of the previous, and they can confront what specialists allude to as the "kickback impact"— social and expert assents for neglecting to adjust to sexual orientation standards. For instance, certain ladies are frequently seen as less agreeable and hireable.

As per another ongoing examination, it's regularly a dread of this backfire, and not an absence of certainty, that keeps numerous ladies from self-advancing. Scientists at Northern Illinois University had a gathering of female understudies compose grant application expositions clarifying why their aptitudes and accomplishments made them the most meriting beneficiary. A few ladies were told the exposition would be unknown while others were told their name would be incorporated. At the point when the activity was finished, the members were approached to state how well they'd performed. The mysterious writers, who didn't need to stress over a backfire, evaluated their accomplishments higher than the individuals who were told their name would be incorporated. For Meghan I. H. Lindeman, one of the scientists who led the investigation, the suggestions are clear: Without any progressions to ladies' dread of backfire, "they are probably not going to effectively self-advance, regardless of how certain they feel," she says.

Likewise with most misdiagnoses, the recommended medicines for ladies' alleged absence of certainty—rehearsing power presents, banishing vocal propensities like "upspeak," disposing of negative contemplations—don't appear to have had any effect. Indeed, a few specialists ponder the certainty hole may unreasonably have generally confident ladies disguising the possibility that they're deficient in certainty.

"I'm beginning to think about whether we could be making the wonder that we should ponder," says Riley Bowles, the Harvard educator.

Eventually, the most concerning issue with the certainty hole hypothesis is that it puts the obligation regarding shutting the sexual orientation hole on singular ladies when the arrangement may rather lie outside their ability to control. "The emphasis on the certainty hole is alarming as it recommends something isn't right with ladies, and that we have to 'fix' them and have them act progressively like men," says Jessi L. Smith, a teacher of brain research at the University of Colorado at Colorado Springs. "This loses the duty and the weight." Smith, who has examined sex standards in the work environment, says that the systems that have the greatest effect in ladies' absence of self-advancement put the onus on organizations, not the ladies who work in them. One basic strategy is for work environments to standardize the act of self-advancement, with the goal that when ladies talk about their accomplishments, they are less inclined to confront the well-recorded kickback. "Start each gathering by requesting that everybody share one thing they've accomplished since you last met," Smith prescribes. "It could be huge or little; it may be business related or individual. The thought is that everybody gets a turn, and that everybody gets the opportunity to characterize what considers an achievement."

Organizations ought to likewise hold workshops that feature for representatives the exploration on the backfire that certain ladies regularly involvement with the work environment, Smith includes. Not exclusively would these trainings make individuals increasingly mindful of their profoundly imbued yet regularly certain sexual orientation predispositions, however they would likewise help generally sure ladies comprehend why they may feel awkward self-advancing.

Ladies can likewise bring issues into their very own hands, for instance by attempting to outline their accomplishments in shared terms. "You would prefer not to exaggerate the 'we' with the goal that you vanish completely, yet you would like to clarify that the work you do and the thoughts you have are useful for the organization," says Riley Bowles. She additionally suggested that ladies follow and verbalize their commitments at work, particularly when filling in as a component of a blended sex gathering. "Individuals are bound to depend on their assumptions and generalizations in equivocal circumstances," Riley Bowles said. "The less straightforwardness there is about the real commitments a lady made, the more potential there is to limit her work."

Normalizing that sort of straightforwardness in the work environment, with explicit strategies and group auxiliary changes, would do unmistakably more to assist ladies with getting their work perceived than any motivational speeches planned for boosting their own certainty.

CHAPTER 4

Why self confidence is required for women?

Ladies in Leadership: Building Self-Confidence

Fearlessness is connected to contracting and advancement choices and there is a generally shared conviction that ladies need self-assurance to take on more noteworthy duties.

Albeit in excess of 60 percent of EHL's present understudies are female, arriving at the C-suite is as yet an issue, as just 17 percent of the school's graduated class possessing senior official jobs are ladies. Not long ago EHL propelled its Women in Leadership (WIL) activity, with the point of elevating authority strategies to encourage different and adjusted workplaces in the neighborliness business.

In mid-November, we arranged the school's first WIL workshop focused on proficient certainty building. We handled this theme since fearlessness is connected to enlisting and advancement choices (Smith, 2013) and there is a generally shared conviction that ladies need self-assurance to take on more noteworthy obligations.

For example, the issue of certainty has kept coming up in the yearly Femmes Leaders boards sorted out by Bilan. The specialists shared stories, affirming that ladies should have been asked multiple times before taking an official activity. Ladies additionally would in general ensure they had all the necessary abilities before taking a vocation, while men acknowledged the activity with a couple of capabilities from the rundown.

There may be a trace of validity in this case. An online investigation of almost one million people crosswise over 48 nations uncovered that, all in all, men had more prominent confidence than ladies (Bleidorn et al. 2016).

Then again, look into likewise shows that in accomplishment situated spaces, there is no proof of a female unobtrusiveness impact.

Truth be told, the hole isn't among people self-assurance, rather the presence of self-assurance. Some way or another, high-performing ladies needed to extend warmth when they were gleaming with self-assurance so as to be compelling, while men just expected to extend self-assurance to practice initiative impact (Guillen et al. 2018).

Here are a portion of the key discoveries from the workshop:

Associations regularly neglect to understand that their authority advancement rehearses depend on instances of men having effectively climbed the positions in commonly male-commanded administration populaces.

Subsequently authority advancement comes down to cloning effective male pioneers. (Vanderbroeck, 2010). Given that ladies can be fruitful in positions of authority in fairly various ways, this model doesn't generally fit them. Pioneers are required to seem certain. Since they are relied upon to be ladylike, ladies who show an excess of "male" conduct, (for example, certainty) are not generally welcomed by their friends at the top since they give off an impression of being "not female enough" and inauthentic. However ladies who show excessively little of this conduct are seen as not appropriate for the top occupation: "excessively ladylike". Accordingly, as long as ladies are in a minority, they are seen as ladies first, and pioneers second. This places ladies in twofold tough situation (Eagly, 2007).

Being a sure and bona fide pioneer implies perceiving that you are separately extraordinary and utilizing it to further your potential benefit.

Expanded mindfulness through the correct criticism enables a lady head to adjust her conduct and correspondence to guarantee that her administration characteristics are effectively seen by the association: an innovator in her actual right instead of a lady chief.

Accordingly, ensure you consider a spade a spade: positive outcomes, which can be estimated all things considered, have the right to be perceived.

Lowliness, similar to narcissism, is a useful initiative quality, as long as it comes in sound portions and doesn't drop into underestimation. Lowliness can be misconstrued for absence of certainty.

Effective ladies pioneers, who have arrived at the top, utilize ladylike models of genuine power and position to show certainty, for example, as moms, instructors and female warriors (Vanderbroeck, 2014). In that manner, they can utilize their distinction furthering their potential benefit. Certainty involves outlook: be the true lady pioneer you need to be.

Why Women Leaders Need Self-Confidence

Leslie Pratch

On January 1, Virginia Rometty will turn into the principal female CEO of International Business Machines Corp. Articles about her have praised her capacity to mix energy, charm, clear correspondence, vital reasoning, and "cool-disapproved" basic leadership. Be that as it may, one New York Times story put the accentuation on the job fearlessness may have played into her prosperity:

Right off the bat in her profession, Virginia M. Rometty, I.B.M's. next CEO, was extended to a major employment opportunity, however she believed she needed more understanding. So she advised the enrollment specialist she required time to consider it.

That night, her significant other asked her,"'Do you figure a man would have ever responded to that question that way?"

"What it encouraged me was you must be exceptionally certain, despite the fact that you're so self-basic inside about what it is you might know," she said at Fortune's Most Powerful Women Summit this month. "What's more, that, to me, prompts going for broke."

Self-assurance is one of the components of dynamic adapting, a lot of practices integral to official achievement that I've recognized in my work surveying administrators for senior positions of authority. In the principal half of 1990s, I headed research at the University of Chicago Booth School of Business examining the more drawn out term character indicators of authority. Among the connections inspected were those among sexual orientation, adapting, and inspiration in the assessment of authority adequacy.

Among the especially striking discoveries of this examination were the contrasts among people on proportions of dynamic adapting. On the off chance that you are keen on the theoretical and exact methodology fundamental the examination, a scholarly article detailing the discoveries can be found here. More or less, we took proportions of adapting, inspiration, and knowledge toward the start of the investigation. Toward the finish of the examination, we surveyed the capacity of these measures to foresee initiative viability as assessed by companions, bosses, and subordinates.

We found that the main measure that anticipated initiative for people the same was a general proportion of dynamic adapting that demonstrates the capacity to react adaptively to pressure and to develop. Be that as it may, this measure was unmistakably more firmly connected with impression of ladies' authority adequacy than it was for men's. What's more, when we separated the components of dynamic adapting, we found significantly more grounded sexual orientation contrasts.

Class 2, a proportion of the preparation to explain wellsprings of disappointment and challenges as far as the outside condition (instead of inside oneself) was emphatically and essentially related with authority viability for ladies however not men. Dismissal 3, a proportion of guarded dubiousness and vagueness, was adversely and fundamentally related with initiative adequacy for ladies yet not men. Classification 4, a proportion of fearlessness and confidence, was altogether related with initiative for ladies yet not men.

Sexual orientation based desires for conduct impact the styles and assessments of pioneers. Ladies are relied upon to show elevated levels of social (mutual) characteristics, including requirements for association, a propensity to act naturally yielding, worry with others, suddenness, and passionate expressiveness. Men are relied upon to show elevated levels of agentic characteristics, those related with acting or applying power, including freedom, decisiveness, self-assurance, and instrumental skill.

Applied to authority, sexual orientation job generalizations propose that female-cliché types of administration are relationally situated and community, while male-cliché types of initiative are task arranged and commanding. To the degree that ladies who are pioneers show a manly style, they intensify their job strife and increment the odds of accepting unreasonably negative assessments.

Male pioneers don't confront an essential job strife closely resembling the contention that female chiefs face since assumptions regarding conduct that is fitting for a pioneer concur to a great extent with convictions about the conduct that is suitable for men. Men are more liberated to complete authority in an assortment of styles without experiencing negative responses in light of the fact that their administration is conventionally seen as genuine. We anticipate that men should show self-assurance, and exactly as expected, men indicated little fluctuation in the proportion of fearlessness. Subsequently, self-assurance didn't anticipate decisions of men's authority.

For ladies, the capacity to distinguish and confront troubles in the outer world transparently and non-protectively anticipated authority past any possibility event. The connection between's fearlessness and initiative adequacy was additionally overwhelmingly factually huge.

Overall, these discoveries demonstrate that ladies must have high confidence and high fearlessness while driving in a collective style so as to be seen as compelling pioneers. To put it plainly, they should be more grounded copers so as to rise above the requirements put on their administration style. Virginia Rometty seems to exhibit these qualities.

WHY SELF-CONFIDENT WOMEN HAVE LESS INFLUENCE THAN SELF-CONFIDENT MEN

This is one of our allowed to-get to content pieces. To access all Ideas for Leaders content please Log In Here or on the off chance that you are not effectively a Subscriber, at that point Subscribe Here.

KEY CONCEPT

Another examination shows that the presence of self-assurance coming about because of superior gives men more prominent impact in their associations. The equivalent isn't valid for ladies, who notwithstanding seeming fearless should likewise show dynamic concern and backing for other people.

Thought SUMMARY

Ladies are as yet a minority in numerous male-commanded callings, for example, building and innovation, just as being a minority in administration positions in many ventures. Past investigations have indicated that ladies in these businesses make some troublesome memories applying a similar impact in their associations. One explanation regularly refered to is that ladies don't seem to have a similar self-assurance as men, which harms their odds of advancement.

The facts confirm that people who venture fearlessness are bound to be given influential positions — particularly in male-overwhelmed callings in which fruitful individuals are self-assured and accomplishment situated. Notwithstanding, the suspicion that ladies don't seem self-assured is an error: ladies in accomplishment arranged spaces venture as a lot of self-assurance as men. The center issue, as uncovered in another investigation, is that anticipating fearlessness doesn't have similar ramifications for people.

In light of an overview of exceptionally gifted PC designs, their bosses and their friends at a global programming advancement organization, the examination initially affirms that high occupation execution expands the presence of fearlessness according to a person's bosses for the two people. Nonetheless, as indicated by the aftereffects of the investigation, a man's fearlessness will expand his impact in the association while a lady's self-assurance won't.

Why this distinction? The examination offers a clarification by uncovering that this sexual orientation distinction in the effect of fearlessness on impact can be moderated through 'professional social direction'.

Genius social direction alludes to the craving to help other people. The consequences of the investigation show that the higher a lady's genius social direction, the more impact she will pick up from her appearance of fearlessness. At the end of the day, it's insufficient for a lady to seem self-assured because of her elite. In contrast to men, she should, what's more, show an inspiration to profit others and to be a decent corporate resident.

The investigation depended on studies of 236 designers, 22 direct administrators and 256 partners; the partners included different bosses and supervisors, peers, and inside customers. The immediate chiefs and the partners assessed the activity execution of the architects. The 22 direct bosses assessed the self-assurance and authoritative impact of the architects. The architects self-assessed their master social direction.

BUSINESS APPLICATION

The way that a lady's self-assurance is perceived and acknowledged in the present work environment is a positive development for more prominent headway balance. Be that as it may, ladies additionally must know about the expert social factor — regardless of whether reasonable or not — on the off chance that they need to be advanced. They need to perform well and furthermore put time in helping other people and being a productive member of society.

This not just places a weight on ladies as far as time and center, however can likewise constrain their reactions to circumstances in the workforce. For instance, ladies may delay more than men to settle on disagreeable choices or voice testing positions, since such choices or positions could affect their professional social certifications. Along these lines, unexpectedly, their necessary professional social practices can hinder their headway in the association.

Organizations that really esteem assorted variety and sex equity ought to know about these limitations on ladies, and find a way to kill any such sex gives that put ladies off guard. Here are a few stages organizations can take:

Choose whether being expert social is an occupation necessity (notwithstanding task execution). Organizations ought to have a rundown of criteria for accomplishment in their association, and explicitly incorporate ace social conduct as a criteria thing in the event that they worth such conduct. Thusly, the activity execution of people are assessed along similar criteria.

Expressly remember genius social conduct for the choice criteria for advancement. Once more, the objective is that people are assessed — for this situation for advancements — in light of similar criteria.

Empower realness. On the off chance that professional social conduct isn't expressly empowered, a few ladies may stifle their genius social inclinations to "fit in" the way of life of the association — which at last outcomes in inner pressure for the person. Organizations ought to expressly support legitimacy, featuring the various ways to accomplishment in their associations.

5 Reasons Why You Must Develop Your Self-Confidence

Have you at any point needed to accomplish an objective so much you couldn't rest? A great many people need to accomplish their objectives however they undermine the significance of self-assurance.

The Merriam-Webster word reference characterizes self-assurance as trust in oneself and in one's forces and capacities. Certainty is characterized as a quality or condition of being sure.

You should be sure about your capacities, characteristics and judgment. On the off chance that you are unsure, it's hard to persuade anybody to be sure about you.

Self-assurance isn't shallow. It's a profound feeling of mindfulness inside you that makes you sure without the garments or cutting edge protective layer we love to cover ourselves in.

I used to be timid. I appeared to be certain at work. Be that as it may, at get-togethers, I was bumbling at firing up discussions or making new companions.

Might I be able to state I was certain? Obviously. In any case, would i say i was genuinely sure? No.

Everybody has a proportion of an absence of self-assurance in them. Be that as it may, we have to arrive at a spot where we are really positive about ourselves with no covers.

How I Became Self Confident

At some point, I chose to build up my fearlessness. I settled on this choice when I understood the open doors I was absent because of an absence of fearlessness. I read books on self-improvement, I joined a Toastmasters club and I stuck around individuals who were self-assured.

My connections improved. I was advanced at work. I had the option to begin one-on-one discussions.

Creating self-assurance isn't discretionary. It is obligatory.

You could inquire as to why you have to build up your self-assurance. You may think just business visionaries or top officials should act naturally sure.

I might want to impart to you five reasons why you should build up your fearlessness.

1. Fearlessness makes you alluring

Would you like to carry on with the life you had always wanted?

Would you like to turn into an individual of fortune?

You should have the option to draw in the correct sort of individuals into your life. You have to figure out how to be appealing.

Individuals are pulled in to self-assured individuals.

On the off chance that you strolled into a room, which of these two individuals would you be pulled in to? The person remaining in a corner with a grin all over or the woman whose head is bowed, gazing down at her telephone. You would be pulled in to the person.

At the point when you are self-assured, you are increasingly alluring.

2. Self-assurance gets you procured for your ideal employments and customers

On the off chance that you were the principle participant at an introduction, OK tune in to the moderator in the event that he wasn't taking a gander at you? You wouldn't tune in. You would turn off in your psyche.

In any case, imagine a scenario where this man was taking part in his introduction. Imagine a scenario where he was sure. He posed the correct inquiries and expressed the words you needed to hear. His persona was locks in. You would hear him out.

In the event that you need to wrap everything up, you have to convey what needs be certainty to your imminent customer. On the off chance that you need to find enlisted for a line of work, you have to communicate certainty to the questioners.

I've been blamed for showing a feeling of pomposity when I go to interviews. Yet, it's gotten me the sort of occupations I imagined about. A questioner would prefer to contract a fearless individual over a non self-assured individual.

3. Fearlessness encourages you focus on things you just dream about

Is it true that you are hanging tight for your large break? Does the existence you need appear to be inaccessible? Self-assurance gives you the guts to request what you need.

I had a fantasy to be an undertaking administrator. Everybody disclosed to me it was incomprehensible and I should adhere to what I knew — building. I had the fearlessness to approach forthcoming bosses for the situation of an undertaking director. I got what I requested!

On the off chance that you need to carry on with the life you had always wanted, you should be sure. On the off chance that you are not, ordinary supernatural occurrences will cruise you by. You won't request what you truly need. Try not to anticipate that individuals should guess what you might be thinking. Inquire!

4. Self-assurance encourages you settle on the correct choices

At the point when you are self-assured, you pick yourself. A great many people who need fearlessness love to please individuals. They don't pick themselves. Since they don't, they settle on an inappropriate choices.

The more you settle on the correct choices lined up with your most profound wants and your basic beliefs, the quicker you will accomplish your objectives.

5.Self-certainty makes you beneficial

You should be profitable and deal with your time admirably. Kill all the superfluous exercises. You can't do this successfully without self-assurance.

Without fearlessness, you will invest energy in exercises that don't assist you with accomplishing your objectives.

The astonishing thing is this activity is done unknowingly. You don't understand you're doing it. I've understood when I don't feel sure about my capacity to accomplish an objective, I sit around idly. I tarry. I do mechanical errands like browsing my messages as opposed to concentrating on the imaginative assignment I need to do.

Why "Have faith in Yourself" Is Bad Advice for Women

In the working environment, ladies can benefit from self-assurance just when they display "ladylike" practices too.

Hopeful ladies pioneers are normally informed that their key to accomplishment in male-commanded conditions is self-assurance. Men have it; ladies don't—which represents the size and willfulness of the sexual orientation authority hole.

In the scholarly writing, as well, study after examination has discovered an immediate connection between self-assurance and impact over others. In the event that skilled individuals with high confidence normally draw in a larger number of devotees than those whose legitimate commitments are smothered without anyone else's input uncertainty, at that point more ladies could become pioneers basically by putting stock in themselves. However, in the event that it were that simple for ladies to get what they merit, would despite everything we be discussing it?

Actually, certainty isn't so direct. It is entirely subjective. Our associates can't peruse our musings (luckily for us). They don't have a clue how we truly feel about ourselves and our capacities. What is important is being seen as self-assured. What's more, this emotional component opens the entryway to inclination, as I portray in another examination co-composed by Laura Guillén of ESMT Berlin and Margarita Mayo of IE Business School.

The investigation uncovered that people have strongly disparate courses for changing over self-assurance into hierarchical impact. The way accessible to ladies is unmistakably increasingly mind boggling, twisting through social generalizations that have an inseparable tie to sex.

Impression of certainty

Going into our investigation, we had a few theories. Since there is no target approach to pass judgment on others' self-assurance, individuals will in general use intermediaries, one of which is execution. At the point when we see somebody who gets results, we are probably going to extend onto that individual the whole authority bundle: fearlessness just as aspiration, status, appeal, and so on. Be that as it may, the envisioned initiative properties we partner with superior workers are profoundly relevant. In male-ruled conditions, the mantle of authority will appear to settle all the more effectively on the shoulders of men, since that is what is as of now natural—and thus expected—inside that specific circumstance.

We estimated that in conditions with not many ladies in influential positions, high-performing ladies can't depend entirely on self-assurance to impel them up the positions. Since sexual orientation generalizations manage individuals' conduct and judgment in a fairly programmed way, ladies are probably going to be relied upon to exhibit further characteristics, as per ameliorating generalizations of womanhood. Specifically, we expected that being a decent authoritative resident, being prosocial, and showing care for the welfare of the association and friends are probably going to be extra, certain yet "mandatory" prerequisites for ladies to accomplish impact.

Our examination

We gathered the information from 236 profoundly talented PC engineers working at a global programming improvement organization. Initially, we had them rate each other's activity execution. They were likewise asked to self-survey their "prosocial direction", for example their degree of worry for others' welfare at work. After one year, we requested that their administrators rate their fearlessness and hierarchical impact.

In accordance with standards in this intensely male industry, just 23 percent of the architects and five percent of the chiefs were ladies.

For the male greater part, there were obvious, direct relationships between's simply the exhibition assessments, saw certainty and authoritative impact. We could follow in the information the procedure by which superior workers were recognized as future pioneers.

For the ladies, things appeared well and good. The relationship between's activity execution and saw self-assurance was there, much as it was for the men. Be that as it may, the last advance—increasing hierarchical impact—was absent by and large. You had some high-performing ladies clearly overflowing with self-conviction—yet who, their chiefs stated, employed next to zero impact, in contrast to their male partners.

Be that as it may, when we considered in prosocial direction—a territory where ladies are characteristically capable—an example developed. Ladies who showed additionally sustaining conduct had the option to parlay superior into hierarchical impact. Ladies who avoided the supporting generalization were denied impact, regardless of how incredible their exhibition.

Unfortunately, ladies in generally manly callings are not yet made a decision by impartial benchmarks (for example execution, fearlessness). Frequently, their greatness will be perceived simply after they conciliate sexual orientation generalizations. For these ladies, at any rate, "Have faith in yourself" is counsel that tends to just a single feature of the test they face – and is in this way deficient.

Takeaways

Organizations that care about sexual orientation equity can find a way to ease aspiring ladies of the uneven commitment to perform passionate work.

To start with, be unequivocal about the authoritative necessities for progress and headway. In the event that being a decent authoritative resident and helping other people is a prerequisite, it ought to be so for people similarly. On the off chance that it is esteemed a "decent to-have" as opposed to an "unquestionable requirement have", ladies ought not be unduly punished for not displaying it. Determination criteria for work applicants ought to be similarly express and straightforward.

Second, be eager to address suppositions of meritocracy. A developing assortment of research shows that expertly aspiring ladies must go through a test of endurance of twofold principles to propel their vocations. They are not acknowledged as pioneers on their benefits alone. Genuine, men also need to try sincerely and demonstrate they can perform. In any case, they never need to demonstrate that they have a place.

What is fearlessness?

Certainty can be depicted as a confidence in one's self and one's capacity to succeed. Finding some kind of harmony between something over the top and too little certainty can be testing. To an extreme and you can put on a show of being arrogant and discover unanticipated impediments when you overestimate your very own capacities or neglect to finish extends on cutoff time since you think little of the time and exertion they require. Simultaneously, having too little certainty can keep you from accepting dangers and holding onto open doors—in school, at work, in your public activity, and past. Anticipating simply enough certainty causes you gain believability, establish a decent enduring first connection, manage weight and address individual and expert difficulties head on.

Brain research Today

The Hewlett-Packard study – 100% versus 60%

Quite a long while back Hewlett-Packard led an interior investigation that demonstrated ladies went after a position just when they accepted they met 100% of the capabilities recorded. Be that as it may, men were glad to apply when they figured they could meet 60% of the activity necessities. As should be obvious, sexual orientation contrasts in certainty are very sensational.

Ladies underestimate their exhibition

Teacher Scott Taylor directed an investigation at the University of New Mexico Anderson School of Management concentrated on how people rate their activity exhibitions. His group found that female administrators are more than 3x as likely as men to underestimate their supervisors' assessments of their activity execution. Then again, the men somewhat overestimated how their managers would rate them.

Ladies belittle their aptitudes and capacities

True to form, ladies neglect to assess their aptitudes and capacities effectively. In any event, when their outcomes are near those of men, ladies still accept they performed lower than the men.

Here are 5 stages to fabricate your fearlessness in the event that you are a lady:

1. Recognize that flawlessness is unadulterated fiction

Flawlessness is unadulterated fiction.

Arielle Ford

Through her philanthropic, Girls Who Code, Reshma Saujani starts young ladies into the tech world. She will probably get one million ladies software engineering by 2020. In 2016, she conveyed an extraordinary TEDx discourse about young ladies: Teach young ladies about valiance, not flawlessness.

In her discourse, she discusses how we as society raise young men to be valiant and go for broke while we instruct young ladies to grin beautiful, avoid any and all risks and carry on. When discussing her understudies figuring out how to code, Reshma told the crowd that young men approach their teacher for help with their code utilizing these words: There's some kind of problem with my code. Young ladies had an alternate methodology – There's some kind of problem with me.

Accepting that you are commendable just when you are flawless is perilous on the grounds that flawlessness doesn't exist. Flawlessness is a psychological jail ladies lock themselves in. Ladies pass on circumstances since they accept they are not ideal for the assignment.

Ladies need to liberate themselves from the should be great and become OK with doing as well as can be expected and be upbeat about it.

2. Quit contrasting yourself with others

We live in the realm of web based life. We take a gander at our companions' posts about extravagant vehicles or popular garments or goes to fascinating spots. It makes us feel poor or discontent with our lives or less excellent or blessed. We contrast ourselves with them and feel terrible. Or on the other hand we see somebody's battle, agony or adversity and like ourselves since we are not the ones experiencing it.

It's called social examination and it might be descending or upward. The two examinations can cause us to disregard an individual's qualities and point of confinement our capacity to sympathize. Upward examinations can make us feel desirous and bring down our confidence.

Try not to contrast your start and another person's center.

Jon Acuff

3. Become mindful of your qualities

On the off chance that you are understanding this, take a bit of paper and record 10 qualities in the following three minutes.

What number of did you really composed? Three, five, seven?

When gotten some information about others' solid focuses, most ladies can check in any event twelve easily, however when gotten some information about their own, they battle to locate a hardly any by any means.

With regards to most ladies, self esteem and self-information is hard to come by.

Ladies need to get mindful of their qualities. Rather than attempting to take a shot at your shortcomings, invest your vitality and time in developing your natural aptitudes, capacities and gifts.

4.   Recognize   and   praise   your accomplishments

The impostor disorder was first distinguished and depicted by analysts in 1978. This disorder makes individuals question their accomplishments and dread that others will uncover them as deceitful.

Not monitoring your qualities is the main contention that powers the development of this disorder. Before you know it, self-question sets in and you start to accept that you are disgraceful of your present place of employment, or advancement, or life.

What you have to do is recall you didn't get to your present circumstance by some coincidence.

Behind your accomplishments is a ton of difficult work, consistent improvement, aspiration and determination. Your own arrangement of aptitudes and capacities carries an incentive to your manager.

5. Screen your negative contemplations

Do you always believe I'm sufficiently bad, I won't have the option to perform, They won't pick me, I will come up short, I am a disappointment?

This is your self-talk talking negative musings. Can any anyone explain why when we talk about a companion we find such a large number of good and constructive viewpoints, however with regards to our own individual, we are basic and judgemental?

The wellspring of this judgemental internal talk could be our folks or instructors or society. Some may think about this idea as inspiration to improve. However, it's not the case in the event that it changes into consistent analysis and judgment.

CHAPTER 5

How to provide self confidence to women?

THE DEFINITIVE GUIDE TO BUILD SELF CONFIDENCE WITH WOMEN

"Simply be progressively sure!"

Your mum likely educated you regarding similarly the same number of times as your companions did.

What's more, amusingly enough, it's one of only a handful scarcely any snippets of data that has risen above the network from the all inclusive community.

In any case, except if you're cautious, building certainty can be one of the very things that keeps you away from getting the accomplishment with ladies you need.

It can take a moderately direct adventure and transform it into an endless thrill ride of splendid highs and hopeless lows.

Lets attempt a little exercise here:

I need you to envision yourself at your generally sure.

I need you to return yourself in the spot in your life where you've recently felt invulnerable like nothing could stop you. A spot where you had all the certainty you would ever need.

It might have been the point at which you understood that young lady you were pursuing, it might have been that night where it was only on with each young lady you saw, it might have been the point at which you won your football stupendous last, whatever it is:

Discover your place of intensity.

How can it feel to you? How can it feel to be there? On the off chance that you haven't got a spot you can review, simply envision a sure form of yourself.

At that point envision the lady you had always wanted remaining before whatever your picture of flawlessness at this time happens to be. It is safe to say that she is blonde? Brunette? Bends? Model dainty?

At that point envision her standing, seeing you, grinning, with that look of adoration and dedication, how can it feel?

And afterward it changes.

Out of the blue it's not cherish any more, it's gradually evolving. First to lack of interest, at that point to newness, at that point to doubt, lastly, despise.

"I don't care for you. You're not deserving of me." She says. "You're not deserving of anything, you're simply poop. You're only a bit of poo. You're awful, you're not cool, you're simply poop at life."

How's everything that certainty functioning for you now?

Better believe it... It's truly harsh.

We've all been there. Also, truly, you're going to feel like poop if something to that effect was to occur. Except if you're superman, your certainty is going to endure a shot.

Yet, what are your musings about what she's said? Do you stay there, floundering in self indulgence or do you acknowledge that she imagines that and proceed onward with your voyage?

In case you're in any way similar to most folks in the network, you've quite recently hit the descending side of the crazy ride.

You've quite recently dove in down that elusive, elusive slant that is going to return you right where you began once more. No certainty, no vitality, no excitement, and you need to begin the way toward building certainty once more.

Be that as it may, this doesn't occur to everybody.

A few people can ricochet back rapidly from something like this and can even step forward in them finding the lady they had always wanted.

What's the distinction?

There's one key component of building genuine self-assurance that is missing from this situation that implies you stall out on this ride.

The people group reveals to you that the best approach to manufacture certainty is playing out a similar activity effectively, over and over.

It says that when you can accomplish a result more than once, at that point you will construct certainty. Furthermore, it can feel like that as well! However, putting together your certainty with respect to your capacity to accomplish a particular result can be hazardous.

Why?

I need you to envision yourself in your preferred bar. At that point you see the young lady you had always wanted. Would you be able to ensure that you can make her like you? Would you be able to ensure that she's going to need to be with you?

No. You can't.

Regardless of whether you were the most amazing individual in the whole world, regardless of whether you were the Dalai Lama, despite everything you couldn't ensure anything.

Why? Since she's an individual.

She's had encounters, translated those encounters, and concoct an entirely unexpected guide of the world to you.

She may despise you in light of the shade of your skin. She may despise you in view of the manner in which you dress.

She may hate you as a result of your stature. She may simply be in a truly crap state of mind; she may have recently observed her ex attaching with another young lady, you don't have the foggiest idea.

You can't ensure this outer result.

Or then again ANY outside result so far as that is concerned.

On the off chance that you construct your certainty on your capacity to accomplish an outer result, you're catching yourself on an unending thrill ride.

You can't presently, or ever will you have the option to, ensure an outer result. Ever.

It is extremely unlikely it's conceivable on the grounds that there are factors associated with accomplishing an outer result that lie beyond your ability to do anything about in light of the fact that they're outside to you.

They're basically not in your authoritative reach.

You might have the option to improve the probability of progress by bookkeeping and getting ready for these conceivable outer components however there will consistently be an opportunity of disappointment.

In the event that you decide to manufacture your self-assurance on your capacity to accomplish a particular result at that point you will ride the enticement thrill ride until the end of time.

You'll be stuck depending on the following large master to give you the most recent bit of innovation to defeat these persistently happening issues that are devastating your certainty.

On the off chance that you study and study and study, you might have the option to arrive at a point where you're ready to get the young ladies you need reasonably reliably, and during this time, you're going to feel quite great about yourself.

Be that as it may, when you can't, it's everything going to go downhill.

Riddle's breakdown in Style's well known book 'The Game' (pg. 193) is an ideal case of this.

He's going around America, enticing ladies, feeling incredible, at that point unexpectedly, a young lady he's keen on returns to her sweetheart and-

"Riddle went calm. He didn't represent ten minutes. At whatever point we asked him an inquiry, he reacted monosyllabically. It wasn't that he cherished Carly, he simply loathed dismissal" (p.181).

From that point, he goes to see his ex. She's shed 15 pounds, has an extraordinary arse

and wont take him back in light of the fact that she's seeing different folks.

He deteriorates.

He goes from compromising a Reverend with a blade to securing himself his loft and going through days stroking off to web pornography.

This 'dark opening sucking up consideration' (p.192) was making due on antidepressants to make sure he could rest.

The thrill ride he's riding draws nearer and closer to the base of its voyage.

He was pondering demise a great deal, contemplating harming himself and accomplishing something ruinous, and suicide –

"At the point when I'm alert, life sucks. It's useless" (p.199).

Puzzle's certainty is based off his capacity to accomplish outside outcomes.

Being 'the world's most noteworthy pickup craftsman' is the wellspring of his certainty and when he doesn't satisfy that picture, he goes totally down slope.

The main thing that had the option to haul him out of that dim, dull spot was a long time of treatment. Does that sound like something you need to decide to bring into your life? On the off chance that you utilize your capacity to accomplish explicit results to for building certainty then this will be your life.

So what do you do? How would you get off this crazy ride and still have the option to get the outcomes you need?

The issue is based around how you esteem yourself.

In case you're seeing outer elements to tell you how great you are, your certainty is going to keep all over and here and there. It's an endless ride.

The key to getting off this crazy ride and building unfaltering certainty is moving how you esteem yourself.

The fearlessness that the enchantment masters have been forcing on you is self-conviction, which is just a single part of self-assurance.

There are two significant parts to building enduring certainty.

Other significant part that they're missing is self acknowledgment.

Self-acknowledgment isn't tied in with feeling great since you're great at this, or can do that, or can get this objective. It's tied in with liking paying little heed to what you should or shouldn't do.

It's about completely tolerating yourself, as you may be, at the present time, and that at this time, you couldn't be something besides what you are, at the present time.

Lets state you were back remaining before the lady you had always wanted once more.

You're standing seeing her grin...

... Looking at her as that grin diverts to a from of despise, and she gives up on you once more. On the off chance that you'd put together your self-esteem with respect to how she responds to you, you're going to feel like crap and your certainty is going to fall through the floor.

Be that as it may, in the event that you put together your self-esteem with respect to how a lot of fun you make in your life and the amount you love yourself for cherishing yourself, at that point you may feel somewhat miserable, however you additionally may feel somewhat cheerful.

Misery would originate from the way that she's not the young lady you had always wanted, however bliss would originate from knowing naturally that...

This young lady isn't really the young lady you had always wanted.

What's more, you didn't squander long periods of your existence with her. You can proceed onward from her and locate the genuine young lady you had always wanted.

Here's something to play with in your psyche:

On the off chance that how you feel when she guides you to fuck off relies upon how you feel about yourself, is it going to be a quicker way to dominance to continue adapting new and various approaches to prevent her from instructing you to fuck off?

Or on the other hand is it going to be quicker to just rest easy thinking about your self? Things being what they are, the unavoidable inquiry, how would you create self-acknowledgment?

Indeed, simply clutch your steeds for a moment.

I will experience and clarify how the issue you're looking here is at the center of pretty much every issue your confronting and afterward I'll give you how you can understand them at the same time.
Step by step instructions to Build Self-Esteem in Women

In a Psychology Today article, specialist, Neel Burton, M.D., proposes that negative messages, physical sickness, unpleasant life occasions or a general sentiment of absence of control in your life can bolster low confidence, as can horrible youth encounters and relinquishment. Low confidence can result from sorrow as untreated despondency can prompt low confidence. Ladies with low confidence may build up an unfortunate casualty mindset, which can make it progressively hard to see the world in a positive way and stand up for themselves.

Depressed people tend to depress everyone around them

The more drawn out a lady endures with constant low confidence, the more vulnerable and incapacitated she may feel with regards to making changes in her musings and practices. Without monitoring it, she may search out individuals throughout her life who strengthen her negative view in regards to herself and people around her. Burton suggests searching out the help of companions or relatives who she can depend on to assist her with beginning to search out the organization of constructive individuals. While it's not important to jettison negative organization totally, it tends to be useful to avoid them until she has a superior handle on her self-esteem.

Negative to Positive

Changing how ladies see themselves is a procedure and a few ladies may require the assistance of an expert to do as such. All ladies can possibly make changes and be fruitful in their lives. Whenever something negative occurs, accept the open door to transform it around into a positive circumstance, as per the article, "Seven Steps to Self-Esteem," distributed on the Oregon State University site. For instance, if your confidence is enduring in light of the fact that you didn't get the advancements you buckled down for, make a stride back and choose what you can do. You may discover new open doors by returning to class and expanding your vocation potential.

Independent

Little encounters can show ladies huge exercises. As opposed to hang tight for her significant other or a jack of all trades to fix the ding in the divider behind the washroom entryway, she can get the spackle and do it without anyone else's help. Little triumphs make a lady feel cultivated and great about herself. This inclination can drive her into going out on a limb and creating expanded self-assurance and regard. In a Psych Central article, Maud Purcell, LCSW, suggests that ladies should remain with their objectives with the frame of mind that they can do it. By acting unquestionably, ladies will start to feel it also. They can likewise focus on other ladies in their lives who go for broke and have a sound feeling of confidence and enroll at least one of them as their coach.

The Doctor is In

Psychotherapy   ,   especially   objective

coordinated treatment, is useful for ladies enduring with confidence issues, as indicated by the article, "Confidence," distributed on Good Therapy.org. Regardless of whether seen as a person, in a gathering or as pet treatment, objective guided treatment can assist ladies with uncovering the explanations behind their low confidence while building up an arrangement to find a way to fortify their feeling of self. For instance, if a lady is aggressive and makes an act of contrasting herself with others, she may feel lacking when she doesn't match her benchmarks. This can influence her confidence. On the off chance that she conveyed a not exactly excellent discourse at her last business related meeting, her specialist can assist her with devising an arrangement to manage difficulties, for example, these in a way that isn't interlaced with her self-esteem.

5 Ways Your Self-Esteem Impacts Your Sexuality

In all honesty, I composed my Master's proposition on the association between masturbation (mentalities and practices) and confidence and self-perception. Most likely there are numerous associations between these pieces of our sexuality, and they happen from multiple points of view in individuals' lives.

This week, I thought I'd investigate (that theory is entirely old now!) at a few different ways individuals' confidence impacts their sexuality (and the other way around). At it's center, confidence is tied in with holding ourselves in regard—loving oneself. Do you wake up every day and love being you? Do you bolster you? We as a whole have confidence needs, in which we want acknowledgment of our accomplishments by our friends, we build up a feeling of capability and have the regard of others. We feel our very own feeling of self-esteem. Here's the means by which these requirements may happen in your sexuality.

1. Sex for the Right or Wrong Reasons

The greater part of us know about the possibility that low confidence can mean poor choices about sex—or the penchant for good choices with a sound confidence, so far as that is concerned. A feeling of amazing confidence will by and large outcome in somebody settling on credible decisions about their sexuality, who they need to engage in sexual relations with, regardless of whether to utilize security, etc. However a few people don't have a solid confidence and will settle on poor sexual choices since they need conviction and quality in themselves, re-think themselves or don't have a solid inner feeling of what their identity is and what they truly need.

A few people truly feel (regardless of whether they are aware of it) that sex is all they bring to the table. They offer it to individuals they would prefer truly not to offer it to, or who don't value their sharing of their body and sexuality since they need to be loved by them and need to develop their confidence. Mindful, true, solid sexual choices rely on the nearness of an invigorated confidence.

2. Certainty and Sexual Self-Esteem

Henry David Thoreau

Confidence is tied in with building fearlessness, preferring oneself, having a sound degree of accomplishment in one's life and picking up the regard of others. Many individuals have some sort of mindfulness, regardless of whether it's psyche, that when they feel explicitly amazing that certainty appears from multiple points of view. Certainty is all around thought about hot.

Numerous individuals feel they are great at sex, regardless of whether they are bad at different things and it gives them a feeling of fearlessness. Individuals who can deliberately sustain their sexual vitality can improve their own certainty and utilize that vitality as fuel to their life the manner in which they truly need to live it.

By a similar token, absence of confidence is typically absence of sexual certainty. That can show up deceivingly as overstated or presumptuous sexual posing.

Get my 4 Tools for Powerful Orgasms PDF Worksheet

I made this asset control with 4 useful assets and activities that will get you into your body and experience more joy!

First Name

Last Name

Email

GET ACCESS

3. Hotness or Over-sexualization?

Ladies are molded that we must be pretty and attractive and men are exceptionally adapted to be explicitly virile and alluring—and to stamp their indents on the bedpost when they "accomplish" another sexual success. There is a major example in numerous ladies of having intercourse, over-sexualizing themselves or utilizing their hotness so as to feel deserving of something or great at (for) something. At the point when your confidence is worked around your provocativeness, sexual capacity or sexual ability, it's based on a place of cards. Maybe for certain individuals it works—it very well may be shallow yet on the off chance that they are great at it and their provocativeness turns into their thing, they can truly pivot their self-esteem here for most of their lives. There is so a lot of media accentuation on how we should look, act, and perform explicitly that this thought of sex = confidence is extremely unavoidable. Eventually, you will require something other than your hotness to build up your self-esteem.

4. Sex for Approval Seekers

Searching for endorsement?

Individuals with low confidence will continually look for endorsement from others, regardless of whether they are uninformed of it. Absolutely for the vast majority who are looking for endorsement, needing to realize you are wanted is significant and it gives you a certainty help. This is obviously, situated in the sense of self and it includes you leaving yourself, thinking you need another person to like you or acclaim you as opposed to you giving that recognition to yourself. It's pleasant to be wanted, and to be helped to remember your longing. In any case, in the event that you NEED it to feel alright, something is amiss.

At the point when we base our regard on outer elements, we are not so much responsible for our lives and that makes us defenseless and effectively misled. It can likewise lead us to act inauthentically or out of honesty.

5. The Desire to Be Good (at Sex)

Living in when we have quite a lot more data about sex is an incredible test for some "sex nerds" who are focused on being as well as can be expected be with regards to sex. These are individuals who love a test of picking up something and learning it well. You go! They will out-perform a great many people with regards to sex since they have truly set aside the effort to figure out how to be great at sex.

Obviously, the flipside of this one is that being "great" may be excessively essential to you. On the off chance that you must be great at everything to be alright, you are most likely missing a ton of a mind-blowing enjoyment experience, and it may likewise show some inner confidence issues underneath all the high-accomplishment A+ sex you are having. However, hello, at any rate you are having A+ sex.

13 Steps to Achieving Total Self-Love

A year ago was a troublesome one for me. I was truly battling with my emotional wellness and was experiencing despondency and uneasiness. Glancing around at other lovely, fruitful ladies, I pondered: How would they do it? How would they figure out how to feel so great?

I needed to discover, and I needed to impart to other ladies who, similar to me, needed to feel upbeat — needed to feel well. Taking advantage of my imaginative vitality, I set out to incorporate an asset anybody could utilize. I asked ladies I knew: What are your mantras and propensities for self-care?

What they revealed to me was both progressive and an all out easy decision simultaneously. On the off chance that I can rehearse them, I realize you can, as well. Here are 13 plans for self esteem that are straightforward practically speaking and multifaceted in their advantages.

1. Quit contrasting yourself with others

We're associated to be aggressive, so contrasting ourselves with others is normal. Be that as it may, it very well may be hazardous. There's simply no reason for contrasting yourself with any other person on the planet in light of the fact that there's just a single you. Or maybe, center around yourself and your voyage. The move of vitality, alone, will assist you with feeling free.

2. Try not to stress over others' feelings

In that equivalent vein, don't stress over what society thinks or expects of you. You can't satisfy everybody, so this is an exercise in futility and will just back you off on your adventure to being the best you.

3. Enable yourself to commit errors

We're told over and over since early on "no one's ideal, everybody commits errors." But the more established you get, the more weight you feel never to come up short. Cut yourself a little leeway! Commit errors so you can take in and develop from them. Grasp your past. You're continually changing and developing from who you used to be into who you are today and who you will be one day.

controlled by Rubicon Project

In this way, disregard voice in your mind that says you should be great. Commit errors — bunches of them! The exercises you'll pick up are inestimable.

4. Recall your worth doesn't lie in how your body looks

This is central! Such a significant number of things on the planet need to divert you from this ground-breaking truth. At times even your own disguised sexism avows your considerations of deficiency. You are important on the grounds that you will be you, not in light of your body.

Along these lines, wear what makes you feel better. On the off chance that it's a ton or if it's a bit, wear what makes you feel sure, great, and cheerful.

5. Try not to be reluctant to relinquish harmful individuals

Not every person assumes liability for the vitality they put out into the world. On the off chance that there's somebody who is bringing poisonous quality into your life and they won't assume liability for it, that may mean you have to step away from them. Try not to be hesitant. It's freeing and significant, despite the fact that it might be difficult.

Keep in mind: Protect your vitality. It's not impolite or wrong to expel yourself from circumstances or the organization of individuals who are depleting you.

6. Procedure your feelings of dread

Like blundering, feeling apprehensive is characteristic and human. Try not to dismiss your feelings of trepidation — get them. This solid exercise can truly help with your emotional well-being. Examining and assessing your feelings of trepidation encourages you to pick up clearness and expose issues throughout your life that were causing you nervousness. That, thusly, can help mitigate a few — if not all — of your uneasiness.

7. Confide in yourself to use sound judgment for yourself

We so regularly question ourselves and our capacity to make the right decision, when more often than not we do know in our souls what's ideal. Recollect that your emotions are legitimate. You're not putting some distance between the real world. You realize yourself superior to any other individual, so be your best promoter.

8. Accept each open door life introduces or make your own

The planning is never going to be ideal for that next enormous advance in your life. The set up may not be perfect, yet that shouldn't keep you away from coming to meet your objectives and dreams. Rather, hold onto the minute since it might never return.

9. Put yourself first

Try not to feel awful about doing this. Ladies, particularly, can become used to putting others first. Despite the fact that there's a period and a spot for this, it shouldn't' be a propensity that costs you your psychological or enthusiastic prosperity.

Discover an opportunity to decompress. Without decompressing and reviving you can put genuine strain on yourself. Regardless of whether it's going through the day in bed or outside in nature, find what encourages you decompress and devote time to this.

10. Feel agony and happiness as completely as possible

Enable yourself to feel things completely. Incline toward torment, revel in your euphoria, and don't put constraints on your emotions. Like dread, torment and delight are feelings that will assist you with getting yourself and at last understand that you are not your emotions.

11. Exercise strength openly

Start expressing your real thoughts. Strength resembles a muscle — it develops the more you practice it. Try not to trust that consent will sit down at the table. Join the discussion. Contribute your contemplations. Make a move, and realize that your voice is similarly as significant as anybody else's.

12. See magnificence in the straightforward things

Attempt to see in any event one lovely, little thing around you each and every day. Make note of it, and be thankful for it. Appreciation not just gives you point of view, it's basic to assist you with discovering happiness.

13. Be benevolent to yourself

The world is loaded with cruel words and evaluate — don't add yours to the blend. Talk generous to yourself, and don't call yourself mean things. Praise yourself. You've made significant progress and become to such an extent. Remember to commend yourself, and not just on your birthday!

Takeaway

Regardless of whether you don't feel especially ground-breaking, consider how far you've come, how you've endure. You're here, at the present time, alive and amazing past your insight. What's more, show restraint toward yourself. Self esteem may not occur incidentally. Yet, with time, it will settle itself into your heart.

Indeed, you may battle, however you'll think back on these minutes and perceive how they were venturing stones on your adventure to being the best you.

Alison Rachel Stewart is a craftsman and the maker of Recipes For Self-Love, a shared activity that praises propensities, practices, and contemplations for self-care and wellbeing. At the point when she's not making customized things for her Etsy store, you can discover Alison composing tunes with her band, making representations, or practicing her imaginative vitality into another undertaking. Pursue her on Instagram.

CONCLUSION

The most significant insight that has come out of this inquiry is that gender-responsive e-government constitutes a normative shift in the idea of governance. E-government can bring women new citizenship rights and opportunities. Its gender transformative potential hinges on measures to translate the vision of gender equality through rules and practices that make governance and democracy work for women.

The move to digital by default in public service delivery is not merely a shift in tools used by systems of government. E-government is increasingly a sine qua non of sound public administration that expands the meaning of good governance. Described as a route to "expanded democracy",147 e-government can be seen as providing new design architecture for governance that can alter the very experience of citizenship.

What this means is that e-government can revolutionize many dimensions of accountable governance, it can make governance more open and inclusive, and give governments the means to reach out to, and promote citizen rights, of women. Gender-responsive e-government can therefore build a democracy in which women matter. A well designed and agile e-government ecosystem can be particularly path breaking for women from the margins, as it accords those without formal documentation the identity and locus standi to become eligible for entitlements upon which their basic needs and rights depend.148

Research studies show that in certain cases, e-government has resulted in alienating the marginalized further from their access to entitlements.149 Social inclusion is often held up in policy documents, but women's empowerment and gender equality are conspicuous by their absence. Without an explicit policy vision and plan of what it can potentially do for women's rights, e-government runs the risk of bypassing women. While the more recent vision of Government 3.0 in the Republic of Korea commits to "transparency, competence, and citizen-oriented services", it is the entitlements approach of the administration in the late 1990s and early 2000s to "actively support informatization as an issue of women's human rights" 150 that may be seen as the critical point that paved the way in the Republic of Korea for positive gender equality outcomes through e-government.

At the national level, multiple expectations are evident in the discourse of e-government, from aspirations to overcome developmental challenges in education, health, skills development, financial inclusion, employment generation, etc., and gaining competitive advantage for national economic progress, to delivering citizen-centric governance. E-government can and should also be seen as a creative and disruptive technique to reach the normative goal of women's empowerment and equality. It should be envisaged and employed as a public policy instrument to deepen democracy so that women can gain full citizenship. The case studies suggest that an a priori twinning of gender considerations and digital techniques in service delivery can address women's needs and interests as citizens, tackling their exclusion from development services and giving them the space to participate in shaping the development agenda. The Community eCentres case demonstrates how an entitlement approach to digital literacy and e-services has direct consequences for women's life chances, while IVR-SERP shows how gender-based violence becomes a critical local governance priority thanks to the rights-based approach in the design of the initiative. Initiatives studied have also pointed to the role of e-government in giving women the 'right to be heard'. The Sreesakthi Portal for example, demonstrates the possibilities for wider consultation with marginalized women across policy areas through a hybrid model even when connectivity infrastructure and mobile diffusion are not ubiquitous. By working through community access points and promoting local groups to share collective experiences, it allows women to shape public opinion through perspectives that are gendered. The Grievance Redress Scheme gives voice to women beneficiaries to express their concerns and assert claims with regard to a benefit transfer programme.

Norms, rules and practices of gender-responsive e-government will need alignment. At the foundational level, women's citizenship must be invoked explicitly by e-government policy, and gender mainstreaming efforts must be institutionalized in all areas of governance, specifically in harnessing the ICT opportunity for women's access to resources and entitlements. Often referred to as process reengineering, these efforts require much more than a systemic shift involving technology and policy; they also call for attention to human resource capabilities in, and cultures of, public institutions.

On the normative plane, the idea of 'citizens at the centre of service delivery' 151 is a mandate that many governments have given for themselves in their e-government plans. Variously, this has included the understanding that the delivery of this promise requires putting more services online, opening up government, collaborating with citizens, accepting feedback on performance and then acting upon that feedback in a timely, effective and efficient manner. Legal frameworks on data protection and the right to information have accompanied policies on broadband connectivity, access to online services, open standards and digital literacy, with institutionalization of a national government agency dedicated to e-government capability. Where there are gender mainstreaming laws and policies and gender budgeting rules, the institutionalization of gender in e-government implementation is stronger.152

In the Philippines, for example, the Republic Act No. 10650 (2014) attests to the aspirations of the government to "to expand and further democratize access to quality tertiary education through the promotion and application of open learning as a philosophy of access to educational services." The law emphasizes that open and distance learning programmes must be delivered using information and communications technology. The case study of the Blended Learning Programme shows how the latter builds on the provisions of the law, offering women fully subsidized access to connectivity and to vocational training, in its service model. E-government policies, the Philippine Digital Strategy and the e-Government Master Plan in the Philippines recognize the role of ICTs for women's empowerment and outline plans of action that are aligned. The country's policies on gender equality and women's rights provide a robust scaffolding to e-government policies and strategies. The government's gender mainstreaming strategy has been institutionalized through the enactment of the Magna Carta of Women, in 2009.

Unfortunately however, the idea that e-government is a means to address the needs and rights of women is not always part of the vision statement of policy. Gender-responsive design in e-government service delivery remains ad hoc in India, despite the ambitious Digital India programme. Key components of the programme such as digital literacy are beginning to be rolled out on a nationwide scale in right earnest, but they are not supported by a vision to equip women for claiming digital citizenship. The policy gap in making e-government gender-responsive is true not only for developing country contexts, and can be a setback for e-government success, especially in its vital role as a catalyst for women's citizen rights.

Gender-responsive practices in e-government certainly depend on strong norms and rules, but institutionalizing gender in e-government also entails wider changes in public institutional cultures. This is a long road, and requires strategies for building across-the-board institutional capacity. In Fiji, interviews with government stakeholders for this research indicated that e-government is viewed as gender neutral and responses show a techno-centric, rather than a sociocultural, understanding of equality of access. When asked about e-government priorities for women, stakeholders shared a view that "technology does not discriminate" and so e-government is about "access on an equal footing". The technicalization of e-government may also reduce gender based thinking to finding simple fixes, as reflected in a comment from an Indian official interviewed for this research: "In Digital India, we are committed to inclusion; this means like accessibility for the disabled, we will also think about women." In the Philippines, despite gender mainstreaming policies, government personnel have varying levels of appreciation for gender concepts and issues. Critical issues such as online violence against women are not adequately covered in e-government capacity-building. Though there are courses offered by agencies such as the National Computer Centre and the Career Executives Service Board in the area of building e-government leadership, most of these courses are silent on women's empowerment and gender equality issues in e-government. In fact, some trainers interviewed for this research insisted that it is difficult to integrate gender in ICT courses.

Even where gender concerns are institutionalized in the broader e-government roadmap through policy and legal measures, the commitment and agility to prioritize gender in implementation design may not obtain automatically. Despite national policy instruments on gender, digital inclusion and e-government153 and recent progress in overall e-government performance, Fiji, for instance, still lags behind in transactional and interactive service delivery possibilities, gendering data collection, targeting service delivery for women and citizen consultation for improving service delivery.

A close congruence between norms, rules and practices within the e-government ecosystem is required in order to promote women's empowerment and gender equality. Without such congruence, women's rights in the expanded democracy that e-government affects are likely to be circumvented.